GRINGOS IN THE AMERICAS

BRIDGING THE CULTURE GAP

Also written by Larry D. Ellis

Forgiveness: Unleashing a Transformational Process
www.theforgivenessbook.com

Radical Worship: What Sunday Morning Cannot Give You
www.theradicalworshipbook.com

Great Connections: Loving with Limits
www.adorationpublishing.com/great-connections-loving-with-limits/

Secrets For a Successful Small Business: What the University will not Teach You
www.thesmallbusinessbook.com

GRINGOS IN THE AMERICAS

BRIDGING THE CULTURAL GAP

Larry D. Ellis, DWS

Adoration Publishing Company
Denver, Colorado USA

Adoration Publishing Company
3767 South Jasmine Street
Denver, CO 80237 USA
Email: info@adorationpublishing.com
www.adorationpublishing.com

Gringos in the Americas: Bridging the Culture Gap

Identifiers:
ISBN: 978-1-950808-00-7 (paperback)
ISBN: 978-1-950808-01-4 (digital)
LCCN: 2019904670

Unless otherwise indicated, all Scripture quotations are taken from the Holy Bible, New Living Translation, copyright © 1996, 2004, 2015 by Tyndale House Foundation. Used by permission of Tyndale House Publishers, Inc., Carol Stream, Illinois 60188. All rights reserved.

Book layout: Adoration Publishing Company
Cover layout: Laurie Cockerell
Graphics copyright © by Discovod/Shutterstock and Andy-pix/Shutterstock

---

1.0.0

Dedication

I dedicate this book to one of my great teachers from many years ago, Señora Florence Tucker (1909–1998). She taught Spanish for many years at my high school in Duncan, Oklahoma. She had earned two masters degree, one in English and one in Spanish. She loved the Spanish language, Latin American people, and their culture. I enjoyed three years of classes with her. She was truly an inspirational teacher. She took many students on summer trips to Mexico to be immersed in both the culture and the language. Each year we had a large Spanish fiesta with dancing and lots of music. Every year, she arranged for a student to come from a Latin American country and be a part of our classes. Her enthusiasm for Latin America was absolutely contagious.

Mrs. Tucker believed you should learn a second language in the same order you learned your first one: first you hear it, say it, read it, and finally write it. In the early lessons, she would pronounce the verb conjugations and the class would repeat them back to her. We used the language lab and recorded our pronunciation and then it could be played back for the entire class to hear. There were giggles, jokes, and lots of laughter in class. In our third year of Spanish, she insisted that no English be spoken, only Spanish. During a quiet reading time in that class, one male student let out a thunderous fart. Mrs. Tucker was working quietly at her desk. She never looked up, but simply said, as she often did in that teacher's voice, *"Repita en español."* The class broke out in total laughter. Nothing else was ever said. Mrs. Tucker was a great lady who loved to teach and had the best sense of humor I have ever seen in a teacher. I thank God she was a part of my life for many years well past high school.

No man is an island entire of itself;
Every man is a piece of the continent, a part of the main;
If a clod be washed away by the sea, Europe is the less,
as well as if a promontory were,
as well as any manner of thy friends or of thine own were;
any man's death diminishes me, because I am involved in
mankind.

English poet and pastor John Donne, 1624

Contents

Acknowledgments

I am particularly indebted to several people who helped me complete this book. I dedicated this book to my incredible high school Spanish teacher, Florence Tucker. I am also grateful to two very good friends who are citizens of Mexico from whom I also have learned a great deal. Mr. José Luis Camorlinga is an engineer and became a great friend who traveled with me on business in Latin America. He taught me a great deal as he worked as my Latin American software sales and support person. He repeatedly told me, "Yes, you clearly do have a gringo accent when you speak Spanish." Dr. Israel Ramirez became a friend during my graduate work. He is also an engineer in addition to serving as a worship leader at his church. Israel carefully went through my manuscript and provided considerable help as I completed this writing project. Both of these great friends live and work in the metropolitan area around Mexico City. A special thanks also goes to Adam Ramirez, who describes himself with a hybrid cultural identity who is constantly transitioning between the Anglo world in the United States and a Mexican bilingual family. Adam has a strong passion to facilitate multi-cultural life-changing journeys.

In addition, several of my local friends, who have a special affection for Latin America, gave me great feedback as I developed my manuscript. In particular, I would like to thank my wonderful mom, Freddy Sue Ellis, my mother-in-law Jeannette Senning, my daughter, Christine Ellis Kosoff, and my good friends The Rev. Barbara Russo as well as Marj Decker who was for a number of years a Christian missionary to Colombia. Each of these friends have helped me bring this book to completion.

Part 1
Step Into a Culture

Introduction

This book is for gringos. I am a gringo. My ethnic origin is clearly Anglo. The roots of my family go back to England and Ireland. My father grew up in Nogales, Arizona, and he occasionally substituted Spanish words for English words in sentences, probably for a bit of humor, but he was not fluent in Spanish. My parents instilled into me the reality that all people from all races were created by God and should be respected and loved even though they might have many cultural differences.

This book is about the many differences between the people from the United States and those from Latin American countries. Its aim is to help advance your encounters and relationships with people from other cultures both in the United States and in Latin America. There are people who have no access to professional education; there are the uber rich; there are those who are educated and work in professional jobs. It is this last group in both cultures with which I am most familiar. In Latin America, some of the historic ways of living and relating are changing as younger professionals move into positions of responsibility. The younger generation does not seem to be as steeped in the historic culture of their ancestors, at least in part due to the vast impact of technology and instant communications which was not available to their parents.

Early on, I would like to discuss several words that are often used interchangeably by Americans. They do not mean the same thing. They are Latino, Hispanic, and Chicano. Like all words, there are the denotations (dictionary meanings) for those words, but they all carry connotations that are assigned by the culture that is using the words. Generally the word Latino refers to all the people in the Latin American countries, including those whose native language is not Spanish. Some speak Portuguese and some speak French. Even so, they have a bond together because there are many similar preferences in the way they live their lives and their geographic proximity. The word Hispanic generally refers to someone whose country was strongly influenced by their history of Spanish colonization and the establishment of Catholicism in the new world by the Spaniards. The term Hispanic would include people from Mexico, almost all of the Caribbean countries, as well as most of Central and South America. That term would exclude people from Brazil. The term Chicano generally is used to refer to people who are living in the United States but who have come from Mexico. Chicano can have a negative meaning to some people; for others it can be used with a sense of pride, often preferred to the terms Latino or Hispanic. In this book I stay with the more broad based term, Latino, for my discussions. I am also expressing culture in the broadest view of culture expressing many generalizations which I feel are legitimate. Bear in mind, there are countless layers of micro-culture in every country.

This book is full of opinions and personal stories of my travels in this region. It does not address anywhere near all the specific diverse exciting nuances that are present in the Latin culture. My observations are wide-spread, but not universal. My major goal in writing this book is to challenge some of the cultural and relational assumptions we might make if our life experiences have been primarily within the Anglo culture.

Latin America has many wonderful people who live life with lots of passion and gusto. The Latin culture is a warm, personable culture that shares many of our American values. It also proudly embraces some perspectives that will likely place some of us well outside our comfort zone, should we not be prepared. Latin Americans have some customs that might seem foreign to Anglo-Americans. There are also many familiar customs and business procedures in the United States that will exist when you are traveling and working in Latin America. If you are flexible, what you learn on a personal level might even help you to expand your business opportunities within the Latin American world. You might also find a new affinity for a new and different culture, cuisine, or lifestyle.

I will share many observations I have made from my experiences throughout Latin America. From these observations, I have formed a few generalizations which, I believe have advanced my understanding in both personal and professional relationships. While these are generalizations, each is based on specific events that have come from my personal experiences. Don't minimize or ignore these perceptions. At the same time, resist applying generalizations to every individual. You will never bridge the culture gap if you embrace some of those stereotypical perceptions about these great people. Make your own observations. The observations you will make as a result of your personal experience will form even stronger impressions, which for you will be even more valuable.

I hope what you read here will pique your interest in Latin America and inspire you to travel there and also embrace new friends from Latin America that live in the United States. As I present some of the issues that will help you plan your travel into Latin America, I encourage you to make a checklist of many things you want to verify about your destination country before you leave home. This planning ahead will minimize the number of potential mishaps in your travels.

I was the president of an engineering software company in the United States for over thirty years. Our first few software sales to Latin American customers were easy to make. We exhibited at several international trade shows that were held within the United States. From time to time, we had visitors to our booth from Ecuador, Venezuela, El Salvador, Colombia, Chile, Mexico, and a few other Latin American countries. We treated them with the same respect we had with our prospective customers from the United States and Canada. We had also been advertising in several national and international trade publications, so these potential customers enjoyed a basic level of familiarity with us. I had also authored several articles in international professional journals that showed innovative use of our software. Because of our international exposure, these early international customers often contacted our company without our having any particular marketing plan unique to Latin America. Rather than actually marketing our software, we were essentially taking orders as they were received at our office.

After a few years, I developed a strategic plan to learn more about the culture, the language, promoting, selling, and providing product support to our Latin American customers. I had studied Spanish for three years in high school plus some in college over forty years earlier. I had visited a few border towns of Mexico and even vacationed in Cozumel, Mexico. For decades, I enjoyed knowing and using a little Spanish, but I had never gone to any great lengths to advance my knowledge of the Spanish language or the Latin American culture. At the onset of moving into the language, several persons from our corporate team went to a Spanish language school for lessons in conversation. This meant we had to move out of our comfort zone. I began by making a few trips to call on current Latin customers and meet some of their professional friends and sometimes even their local competitors. I graduated from the school of hard knocks with respect to learning the language, foreign travel, foreign marketing, foreign laws, embracing foreign cultures, incalculable government and industrial bureaucracies, lawsuits, and collections.

Management of all productive enterprises is an ongoing learning experience domestically, and the same goes for doing business in Latin America. I will share many personal experiences that made an impact upon me over the years. Whether you want to become an experienced vacationer in Latin America, launch a new business work there, or simply have more productive encounters with Latin Americans who live in the United States, I hope this book will serve to give you guidance as you take off.

Cultural Customs Are Different

Never project your customs and expectations onto other cultures. Just as New Yorkers, Houstonians, Denverites, and Montanans are different, customs within Latin America will vary from country to country, state to state, and city to city and certainly from individual to individual. Make every attempt to check your cultural expectations with your baggage when you travel out of our country. If you are a guest in another country, it is wise to adapt to their local culture. Learn to enjoy the discovery of a culture different from your own. If you are in Latin America, do not embarrass your host by making a spectacle of yourself insisting that food, etiquette, and everyone's behavior be as they would be at home. Strive to build long-term, mutually beneficial relationships.

Latin Americans seem to have more of a strong sense of national collective identity on both the cultural and business levels than we do in the United States. They tend to be less individualistic in their visions and plans. Believing we know how all people should always behave will only lead you to a sad, incorrect devaluation of another's culture. Do not remain bound by your own limited cultural values. Should you do this, you will likely never build any new friendships with people across the culture gap. Instead, learn by reading, from your friends or from others who have traveled there, and particularly from your own personal observations as you find yourself immersed in another's culture.

Being different is not being wrong. There is an indeterminate fine line between cultural differences and moral value differences. Be discerning of differences, but do not be judgmental about the differences you observe. Some people assign a moral value to all actions. This perspective implies, "My way is right and all other ways are wrong," only because they are different from my ways. If both parties from differing cultures have integrity, it is possible to cross all cultural differences. If you are fortunate enough to establish long-term relationships with friends with a different ethnic background from your own who prove to be people of good integrity, you will find great personal satisfaction.

Many concepts assumed to be politically correct in the United States will not be present in Latin America. You will not find many gender neutral restrooms, women priests or pastors, discussions about global warming, or gender-neutral references to God. You will not hear the term Happy Holidays during the Christmas season. You will hear *"Feliz Navidad."* Women with strong personalities and tendencies toward extroversion might be perceived as pushy.

You can offend people out of ignorance of their culture. For example, should you hold your hand out horizontally, and ask, "Isn't your grandson about this tall?," you may have just insulted him and his family. Holding your hand horizontally is how some people in Mexico refer to the height of animals. Proper etiquette for these people is that a person's height is signified by holding one's palm in a vertical position. This custom is true primarily among the older people. Many people, especially in their forties and younger do not pay attention to the position of the hand.

The majority of Latin people do not want to make waves in their relationships. Many people in these cultures are much less assertive than Americans and will avoid conflicts, certainly on a personal level. There is a widespread respect, sometimes even fear of persons in authority. The patriarchal system is alive and well throughout the region. Almost all middle and upper managers are men. Women are assuming more and more professional roles, but it is nowhere as commonplace or acceptable as it is north of the Mexican border. Men are expected to treat women with great respect and courtesy, which might even seem patronizing by our current cultural standards. Also, young people are expected to treat older people with great respect and courtesy.

In the United States, when we use the word family, it generally means you, your spouse, and your children. In Latin America, it has a much broader relational definition. It means all your relatives—your parents, grandparents, children, grandchildren, nieces, nephews, uncles, aunts, cousins, sometimes even their families. Family gatherings are not typically held once a year for reunions, rather families enjoy frequent times together unless there is a major geographic separation. Even here in the United States it is common for Latino Americans to have weekly Sunday parties with all their extended family.

Unless the business has been strongly influenced by American management, smoking is widely permitted within the workplace in many countries. It is common to work in an office where fifty to eighty percent of the employees smoke throughout the work day. The exception to this is Mexico City, which has enacted strict laws against smoking inside certain buildings. In the Dominican Republic you can smoke as soon as you exit the plane and wait for your luggage. Few restaurants have non-smoking areas. In many instances, there are no significant accommodations for disabled persons. Many buildings have no elevators, no ramp entrances, and no handicapped restrooms. Reserved parking places for handicapped persons are virtually non-existent. In some remote locations, you can lift the land-line telephone receiver and not get a dial tone or operator for several minutes.

Latin America is one of the few places where a 5' 11" person can feel quite tall and spend the majority of his time looking down rather than across at his associates. Do this in an affirming way, not applying any sense of power to which you might be tempted. Being taller does not really make one more powerful, and you would not want to imply otherwise.

Almost all engineers are young. There does not seem to be any middle age management. Many *jefes* are young and placed in important private and governmental engineering management positions. This is probably because there has been a significant increase in higher education in many of the countries. As graduates develop expertise in needed areas of commerce, they find opportunities for positions that have not always been in existence.

As you personally discover more and more of these differences, do not be surprised if a number of your observations challenge you to adapt some of their style and apply it to the way you live. Our fast pace, cut to the chase, get to the bottom line approach does little to nurture trust and long-term love and respect. Some of us might do well to slow down our frenetic pace of life. Accept these differences of lifestyle as a gift.

Part 2
Traveling in Latin America

Entering the Country

You must have proof of your citizenship when you travel anywhere outside the United States. A few countries might permit you to enter with only a birth certificate, but the best proof is always a current passport. A valid passport will also make your reentry home an easy process. Some countries require your passport be valid for at least six months after your expected date of departure from their country. Plan ahead. Always keep your passport on your person, especially when you are out and about. Never place it in your checked luggage or leave it in your hotel room. Always pack a photocopy of your passport in a separate place from your original. While no one would treat this copy as an actual passport, it can be a great help in the event yours is stolen or lost while traveling abroad. The local American Embassy can assist you with this issue should the need arise.

When traveling overseas, a visa does not mean a credit card; it is a document permitting you to enter a country. There are many types of visas. Some are simply for touring the country. For entrance into a country to conduct business, many Latin American countries require a business visa issued by their embassy or consulates within the United States prior to your entering their country. Some are valid for only thirty days; many are typically valid for one year. It is common to pay a fee of $60-$100 for this business visa. Requirements for a business visa are typically a current U.S. passport, passport photos, a letter on company letterhead explaining your business purpose for travel to their country, and sometimes photocopies of your tickets or travel itinerary. A business visa can be a separate document, but is generally a stamp in your passport provided by the department of immigration of the foreign country. Sometimes certain vaccinations are required. If you are required to get a visa in advance of your arrival, aways allow two to five business days to get the visa, if you are working in person with the embassy or consulate. If you are working through mail and telephone, it will take considerably longer. Generally fax signatures are not acceptable for such applications. Consulates almost never accept credit cards for such services. For non-business travel, you generally do not need a visa in advance. Your passport will be stamped with a visa as you clear immigration upon entering the country. For precise details regarding visas check with the airline, your travel agent, or U.S. state department website (https://travel.state.gov).

If you are expanding your business market, it can also be a benefit to know personally the closest Consul General or Ambassador from the country where you will be traveling. You can always contact these officials directly, but your reception will be much warmer if you can be introduced by someone who knows him or her or if you can identify some mutual acquaintance that you may discuss. Many times, representatives of the country desire to assist in international trade with the United States. The consul will not have much authority over government agencies outside his own, but he will know important people who have relationships with public and private sector leaders in his country. Many times these friends have the knowledge and authority to cut through great amounts of red tape when needed.

Always check with the State Department for any travel advisories about your destination. Advance planning is important, but the acid test of your preparedness is when you are talking to the immigration officer at your destination. If you are not prepared when you arrive, you will be completely at their mercy. They are not particularly merciful. Your urgency for resolution of any problem will not be compelling to them. Find out what your particular entrance requirements are before you leave the United States. Plan ahead.

Upon arriving at your destination port of entry follow the signs to *"Aduana"* (customs). The first stop will be the immigration officer. The immigration agency controls who is admitted to the country. The officer will review your passport and your business visa, if needed, and any other required documents. If everything is in order, you will receive a stamp in your passport and permit, and then you will be instructed to proceed to the baggage area to claim your luggage. At this point you have legally entered the country. After collecting your luggage, proceed to customs. Customs agencies control what you can and cannot bring into the country. When you reach customs, you will present your customs declaration. This is a form provided to you by your airline. Read it carefully and make certain you follow all of its instructions. If you are bringing anything that exceeds specified dollar values into the country, you will have to list the items and possibly pay an importation tax (duty). If you are bringing in only samples of your products to be given away, you can declare them as no commercial value and most likely avoid any duty.

As you near the exit to customs in many Latin American countries, you will likely see what looks like a stop light with a push button. You will be asked to press the button. If you get a green light that indicates *"PASE,"* the contents of your luggage will not be examined. You will be passed through customs in only a few seconds. If you get a red light, be prepared for a growth experience. The customs agents might first take an x-ray of your baggage contents. Then they might ask you to open each bag or box and require a detailed examination. You can easily spend fifteen minutes to an hour with this process, assuming you have no problems. Most agents process hundreds of national and foreigners each day. They would probably prefer you to pass through and not have to solve any problems with you or your documents. Plan ahead. Either prepare your paperwork before you arrive at this desk or be ready to deal with more time-consuming issues or even less-desirable actions by the agents. I always heave a sigh of relief, once I have passed through both immigration and customs.

Traveling with Children

Many countries will not permit the entrance into or leaving a country with a minor child without a notarized affidavit from the absent parent. If your spouse is no longer living, you need some proof of this. If you are taking minors who are not your children, you will need a signed affidavit from both of their parents. The purpose of this is to prevent trafficking children into nations where there is a market for them. At present, almost without exception, all travelers must present a valid U.S. passport for international travel. This rule applies regardless of age, including infants and newborns. Currently, all U.S. children under the age of sixteen must apply in person for a U.S. passport with both parents being present along with the appropriate documentation. Passports for children are valid for five years, where for adults they are valid for ten years. As with all unfamiliar procedures, it is the responsibility of the traveler to know all these matters in advance, before you head to the airport. Plan ahead.

The adults who are supervising the children must carefully manage their passports and any other important documents at all times. Constant vigilance of personal security for children and youth is critical when you are out of the country, just as it is when traveling within the States.

Airline Flying

When possible, make all your flight reservations and ticket purchases before leaving the United States. Air fares are often less expensive if you buy tickets in the States rather than abroad, even for flights internal to the country being visited. Do not be surprised if there are special restrictions. Fare non-refundability except by the issuer of the ticket (i.e., your travel agent) is quite common. Some fares include checked baggage and seat assignments; others do not. Be certain you know and understand your restrictions before you purchase your ticket.

Generally, airline counters are only attended close to the times when flights are arriving and departing on that airline. This is true even at large, foreign metropolitan airports. Many airlines will let you check your baggage only between specified times before the flight. If you arrive at the desk too early, you will have to wait. If you are late, they may not let you check anything. These restrictions are not in place to irritate you. The agents at the counter do not create these rules. They may be in place for reasons of security or double-duty demands placed on the staff. If you arrive more than two hours before departure time, certainly expect to wait to check your luggage. In smaller airports where staff size is limited, you must show up for check-in at least an hour and a half before departure (not thirty minutes as is common at home). Many airlines in the smaller cities close their check-in counters thirty minutes before the flight so the ticketing agents can service the luggage. If you arrive less than thirty minutes before the scheduled departure time, it is likely you will not be allowed to board the flight. Plan ahead.

After checking in and receiving a boarding pass, you might go to a gate where there is no indication of either your flight or your airline. Many times there is not a dedicated gate but a large hall where you will wait with many other passengers for an announcement of your flight boarding. Gate changes at large airports out of the United States seem to be more common than in the United States. Always keep your eyes and your ears open when traveling. Plan ahead. Patience is a virtue.

During my international adventures to and from Latin America I encountered frustrating moments and a few surprise. Even now, I get a little rush as I recall the events.

Mexico

On my first solo business trip to Mexico, I experienced quite a surprise. I had to change from the international flight I had taken into Mexico City to an outbound domestic (within Mexico) flight to another city. My baggage was not checked through to my destination from my originating airport. No one told me this was going to happen either. As I walked through the international arrival baggage claim area, it occurred to me to look for it, just in case it was not transferred. Sure enough, there it was setting in a pile of unclaimed bags. It later dawned upon me that one always accompanies one's luggage through customs when entering a country. Only then can the airlines recheck your bags to your final destination.

I picked up my bags and proceeded through customs. I presented my passport and my filled-out customs form provided by the airline. The immigration agent stamped my visa in my passport. That experience was uneventful. After exiting the customs area, I carried all my three bags what seemed to be a distance of five miles to the *Aeromar* check-in counter. I was glad my connection was not tight so I was not rushed. I navigated through a large and unfamiliar terminal building. When I arrived at the counter, I was also glad there were no lines. I was relaxed because there were still two and one half hours before my next departure. I handed my ticket to the agent, placing my luggage on the scales at the counter. He then advised me it was too early for me to check my bags. He said to come back in a half hour. He could not check them until that time. This inconvenience was not because the agent was lazy. He was complying with the established airline policy over which he had no authority to override. He simply could not accommodate my personal preference.

I then dragged them to the closest available bench and waited for the time to pass. Of course, when I arrived precisely at the appointed time, there was a long line that took about forty-five minutes to go through. When I finally checked my bags and received my boarding pass, I was instructed to go to a particular gate at the end of a specific concourse. I passed through security, climbed the steps up to the concourse, and walked to what I believed would be the gate. When I arrived, it was not actually a gate. It resembled a large waiting room with three or four hundred seats. Restaurants, newsstands, and small shops surrounded this area. There were two large signs, both above their respective door at one end. On each sign a single flight number was listed with a time. Naturally, my destination city, my flight number, not even my airline was listed. There were many passengers roaming the hall. This surprise was a little unsettling to me.

The loud public address system was rapidly announcing flight information in Spanish. I finally heard my flight number announced, but it is not listed on either of the signs. Learning to understand flight numbers in Spanish is important. Printed signage might not be as prevalent as it is in the United States. After inquiring with several boarding agents guarding the doors, I learned through which door I would eventually leave. I then remained immediately next to this door and tried to locate someone else who would be on my flight. After querying three or four persons, I found one. From that point on, I decided to keep him within earshot until we were on the plane. Finally the moment came, and we heard the official announcement. We walked out onto the striped lanes on the pavement outside of the terminal building. This lane led up to an aircraft that was a lot smaller than I had expected.

After boarding the flight, as I leaned back into my assigned seat, I noticed the right side of the back of my seat was broken. It was not attached to the bottom of the seat. It wiggled all around substantially. When I pointed this out to the flight attendant, she gave me a different seat on the plane. She did not seem alarmed or concerned. There were several other open seats on the aircraft. There was no stereo music, no Wi-Fi, no beverage, no movie, nor an in-flight magazine. That flight lasted about forty-five minutes. I felt quite relieved as I deplaned. When I entered the terminal, my friend was waiting for me at the baggage claim area and greeted me with a large smile, warm greeting, and a strong bear hug. I claimed my bags, and he took me to my hotel. I had actually succeeded in my first international flight connection, but not without a few new experiences.

Venezuela

It had been a long tiring week in Caracas, Venezuela. I had been exhibiting our software at a large telecommunications exposition at the *Poliedro de Caracas*. I had spoken almost no

English in a week. I deliberately attempted to reconfirm my return flight reservations on the night before my departure. One of the airline phone numbers did not answer. The other answered with a message stating that they were closed, and there was no need for reconfirmation. Because I had an 8:30 a.m. departure to return home, I arose at 5 a.m. I was told to arrive at least ninety minutes before departure. By setting two alarm clocks and ordering a wake up call, I was certain there would be no problem. I dressed, paid the hotel bill, skipped breakfast, and departed in a hotel taxi at 6:05 a.m. After an enjoyable taxi ride down to the coast, I arrived at the Caracas airport at 6:30 a.m.

I was greeted with a plethora of people at the terminal building. Skycaps came to assist me like you used to experience in the States. The first line that I was to enjoy was one that would admit me to the airline check-in area. I did not receive my boarding pass at this location. We departing passengers lined up beside the four-foot tall glass fence, where all the baggage check and ticketing occur. Probably sixty persons were in this line. I was there for ten to fifteen minutes with no activity, then ten or twelve persons would be admitted. This wait was for thirty minutes until 7:05 a.m. The skycap asked if I wanted him to remain with me, and I said yes. We talked about many things until we were admitted to the check in area.

Once inside that area, we stood in our second line with another forty to fifty people to have our pre-immigration check of our documents by the airline. The next line had only about twelve persons, all waiting for the x-ray of our baggage that would eventually be checked and loaded onto the plane. Each piece was dutifully examined. I had to open my trade show booth crates for an inspection. After they were approved, all checked bags were sealed shut with a strong durable Saran-wrap-like clear plastic non-stretch tape, wrapped over and over. Later, I learned this was not to protect my contents from being stolen, rather to secure the bags, confirming these had been x-rayed and passed through security. Now, nothing could be added to the bags.

The fourth line contained only eighteen people in front of me. We were waiting for one of the three ticket agents who would check our bags for the flight and give us our boarding passes. This line went relatively fast—about fifteen minutes. When I arrived at the counter, the agent welcomed me with a friendly greeting in English. After one or two questions, when I responded in Spanish, he changed to Spanish. He even commented on how good my Spanish was. This type of comment must not be taken too seriously; it is quite common when foreigners try to communicate in Spanish. They want you to feel good about your language skills and have a pleasant memory from your visit.

Because I had intelligently placed one of my two excess bags inside another trying to save an excess baggage fee, I still had the privilege of enjoying an additional line to pay the $46 excess weight baggage fee. Only one other person was in this fifth line. He was somewhat frustrated, because his VISA credit card had been declined, and he was trying unsuccessfully to get the agent to call the United States for authorization. When it was my turn, I also paid with my VISA. There was no problem with it, but the agent suddenly left, telling me not to leave without my receipt. He was gone for five or six minutes and returned from the back room with a computer printed receipt. This friendly ticket agent then pointed me to my next line. I was advised by my skycap to tip the United agent about $15 USD to ensure my bags would actually be checked to Miami and then Denver. He smiled and readily accepted my *propina* (tip). After that experience, I moved to a new line to pay several thousand *bolívares* (approximately $11 USD) for the departure tax to the

Venezuelan government. I was glad to see there was only one other person in front of me. After paying my money, the agent gave me a triplicate copy of my tax payment form, which I had to fill out with all the required information for immigration.

I asked where I would find *puerta* 14 (my departure gate). He pointed in the direction, but told me I would first have to go through immigration. I went to the stand where the two officers were working, only to see there was an incredibly long line—so long it went the entire length of the ticket counter with approximately fifteen check-in stands. This line was so long I had to exit the secured area behind the glass fence that had first kept me out of the ticketing area. I walked back and forth through the line trying to see an alternative. There must have been eighty or ninety people in line. Always plan ahead. Patience is a virtue in this situation.

There was a distinguished Venezuelan couple in their late sixties behind me in the line. After approximately twenty additional people joined the line, a remarkably loud, pushy, American woman and her friend sized up the problem. They decided to simply cut in line in front of the couple. One of the couple then told her no. The lady was loud and said, "Okay, you can go in front of me. After all, we are all going the same place anyway." The rest of the persons behind them in the line said nothing. The Venezuelan wife then said, *"Ah!, Americana!"* I then exchanged looks with the lady—communicating my deep regret for such insensitive, selfish behavior. Although this line was long, it moved quite quickly. I was thrilled I had finally advanced to the front of the line. The officer looked at my departure tax receipt and kept one of the copies. He then pointed me to the next line. Line seven was particularly memorable. I had two lines from which to choose for my carry-on baggage to be x-rayed. Another airport employee quickly made the decision for me as to which line I entered. I placed my notebook computer, bag of gifts, and other paperwork on the conveyor belt and emptied my pockets of keys, change, and anything else that historically sets off those precious metal detectors. I was quite relieved seeing I still had ten minutes before my scheduled departure time. I now saw the sign to gate 14; it was not far down the concourse.

Somehow, I had missed the sixty to seventy people gathered in front of what was the "real" immigration officer. There were no well formed lines, only moderate chaos. My local *Americana* was repeatedly making comments about the situation–none of which seemed to accomplish any changes to her liking. Impatience was her hallmark.

Finally an agent for United Airlines eventually began asking for hands for those going on the Miami flight. She let us skip ahead to the great frustration of others. A quick look at my passport was all she required, and I was on my way to the gate. I was quite relieved. At the gate, I was greeted by my eighth line. The airline was x-raying all carry-on luggage a second time. Many of the passengers had already boarded the plane. As passengers were boarding, the agent asked me many questions such as, "Did you ever leave your bags at any time at the airport?" and "Has anyone given you anything to take with you on the flight?" After answering these questions to his satisfaction and getting my carry-on bag re-examined, I was ready for my ninth line. This was the final line into the jetway to board the flight. I noted the time. I sat down into my assigned seat at 8:22. Three or four others entered after I. The door was quickly shut. We were backing out of the gate at 8:25 a.m. This was the second and final flight to Miami from Caracas for the day. The next one was early tomorrow.

The lesson to learn from these experiences is plan ahead–way ahead. The airlines told me to arrive one and one half hours before departure. I planned for two and should have planned for four or five hours to have a comfortable margin of time. This check-in experience in no way resembles those you might have when flying within the United States or Canada, even if you are traveling with a well established domestic carrier and assisted by one of the "owners" of the airline. The unleashed bureaucracies in the name of security completely amazed me.

Mexico Again

On another occasion, my wife and I were returning to Denver from Morelia, Michoacán. As always, we had planned to arrive early to avoid any problems. After a wonderful business trip there, we were anxious to return home on a certain day, because we were leaving again for a scheduled birthday party a thousand miles to the west. We had only one day of margin at home before we had tickets to leave again.

At the Morelia airport terminal, we had a another new learning opportunity. We discovered that it is possible for airport authorities to close the airport during the middle of the day for two or three hours or more. Scheduled flights may be canceled or delayed for many hours causing you to miss connecting flights. That is what happened to us. The management shut down the only active runway for maintenance. There was no advance notice, nor was there any suggestion as to how many hours the airport would be shut down. There was no reason given for the shutdown; we simply observed heavy machinery being moved onto the runway. All the tears and urgent negotiations with the ticket agent were to no avail. Ticket agents have no authority in such matters. Agents do not respond positively to gringo impatience. We eventually left the airport with our friend and discovered that a karaoke bar can be a fun place to spend several unscheduled hours. We were not able to get a flight out of

Morelia until very late that evening, and we were fortunate to find a flight from Mexico City to Denver even later that night. We made it home quite late, but we were able to fly out for the big celebration. My parents, who were watching our kids, were quite relieved. If we had planned for a little larger margin of time before we left home, it would have been better for us. Plan ahead better than we did. Learn to turn your exasperation into patience. This transformation will serve you well.

Private Flying

As an alternative to the airlines, if you are a licensed pilot, you can fly a privately owned aircraft into Mexico. The Aircraft Owners and Pilots Association (www.aopa.org) provides many great resources to help pilots plan their trips. Many safe private and corporate flights are made daily between cities in the United States and Mexico. However, there are a number of issues you should address before you depart in private aircraft.

Detailed pre-flight planning is always critical, and even more so when you are traveling out of the United States. You must plan your flight itinerary carefully, calculating flight times between stops to refuel. You must select an alternative airport and plan for enough fuel to get there in the event of an emergency. Mexico City has an actual elevation of 7382 feet above mean sea level. That fact alone, should make any pilot give serious thought as to whether or not such a trip would be prudent in light aircraft.

All licensed pilots need to understand the concept of density altitude. Density altitude is essentially the altitude at which that aircraft thinks it is flying. As you go up in elevation (altitude), the air always gets thinner. The thinner the air, the more degraded the aircraft performance will be on the lift provided by the wing and in some cases the performance of the engine. Reduction in air density can make some aircraft's performance so poor that they cannot safely take off or maintain altitude, especially if the aircraft is a bit heavy. All aircraft have some service ceiling, or maximum altitude they can be safely flown.

Just as an example, for Benito Juárez Airport in Mexico City, with an air pressure of 29.92 in Hg (inches of mercury), 85 degrees Fahrenheit temperature, and a dew point of 65 degrees, the density altitude would be 10,953 feet. Since there are mountains all around the city and given the fact that an approach to a major international airport would have to be two or three thousand feet above ground level, your aircraft would need to perform well at 14,000 feet. Many light aircraft cannot meet this requirement. In addition, U.S. Federal Regulations require pilots and passengers to be on oxygen when you rise above certain elevations, unless you have a pressurized cabin properly maintaining air pressure. As long as the entire route of your flight is considerably below your service ceiling your aircraft performance should be fine.

After your flight planning is complete, you will file a flight plan with the Flight Service Station and check both the weather forecast, reported weather enroute, and any special notices to airmen. Finally, you must perform a visual inspection of the aircraft and fluid levels including the fuel level inside the fuel tanks before take-off. A conscientious pilot uses a detailed check list for this process, because no one's memory is perfect. There should be no exceptions to any of these procedures.

I have had only one experience piloting a private aircraft into Mexico. I grant you my experience was not typical. It was full of surprises and unplanned new adventures. Years later, these memories are still locked into my mind as if all this happened yesterday. I believe you will see why.

It was supposed to be a fun trip for a week-long vacation in Mexico City. I completed my pre-flight planning and verified the data on my aircraft. There were no concerns on any of these issues discussed above. Two good friends decided to accompany me on this trip. With hundreds of hours of flying time and a commercial pilot's license including mountain flying training, I was looking forward to my first adventure flying internationally. We flew from Denver, Colorado, to Laredo, Texas, with no surprises, and we stayed there overnight. The next morning, I filed the flight plan for the rest of our outbound trip. We flew from Laredo across the Rio Grande River. I spotted the Nuevo Laredo airport about two minutes after takeoff. I had been taught that English is the international language used for aircraft controllers. I called the Nuevo Laredo tower and requested landing instructions. I received no response. I called back a second time repeating my aircraft identifier number and requested permission to land at the airport. I still did not receive any response from the tower controller. I could see the airport right in front of me, but you do not land at a controlled airport without advance permission. I called a third time in the same manner, and then received a one word response, "Approved!"

In the states, there is absolutely universal content in air traffic clearances for landing. You are given explicit permission to land, an assigned runway on which you must land, an altimeter pressure setting, and the direction and speed of the wind. This moment was the first of many growth opportunities for me as a pilot in Mexico. I saw no other aircraft on approach, so I took the apparent, flexible attitude of "When in Rome, do what the Romans do." I landed the aircraft safely, and taxied up to the terminal building to go through immigration and customs.

As I walked up the steps, I saw the security guard sitting in a chair, reading a newspaper. I saw the date on the newspaper was three days earlier. He politely directed me to the counter where I could pay the appropriate fees for landing and receive my visa and other required documentation for entrance into Mexico. The immigration officer's work space resembled that of a bank teller, except there was a grill between the agent and me.

He spoke English and was quite cordial. The fee was minimal, only ten or fifteen dollars. He happily took U.S. dollars in payment.

I returned to my aircraft and requested clearance for takeoff. Again, I expected a full report of detailed instruction for my takeoff as is always the case at controlled airports in the United States. Once again, I received a one word response, "Cleared!" With that clearance, I taxied to the active runway, took off, and climbed to a comfortable altitude of around six-thousand feet. I continually reviewed my aviation charts and had no planned stops for the flight into Mexico City. I had checked reported enroute weather before I left my flight origin in Laredo, Texas, and everything seemed in good order. I had filed my international flight plan under visual flight rules before leaving Texas.

Although I have never been in Monterrey, as we flew high over the city, I thought it would be a place I would love to visit sometime in the future and sharpen up my Spanish proficiency. The scenery below was exquisite. There were beautiful hills. Since I lived in Colorado, these were not mountains to me, but they were still beautiful. I enjoyed monitoring the aircraft radio traffic as we passed through the Monterrey area. Not all of the conversations sounded like American English to me.

This trip was in the days before GPS was widespread in private aircraft, but current radio navigational aids operated just like they do in the states. These radio facilities seemed to be spaced farther apart than we would see at home, and they also have a number of what are called NDBs (non-directional beacons). NDBs are from a much earlier technology, but they are still used in a some locations, even in the United States. They are much cheaper to install and maintain than the more sophisticated systems. They also are much less precise in the information they provide to a pilot.

I was carefully monitoring my fuel consumption, switching tanks at the appropriate times to keep the weight in the wings properly balanced. I began to notice there were many more cloud layers than I had expected. We continued onward between layers, and then we developed a problem. I noticed our fuel pressure suddenly went to zero. Without adequate fuel pressure, the engine would soon shut down. Being trained for such an event, I immediately switched tanks and the fuel pressure returned to normal, and all was well. All was well, except after a quick calculation of remaining fuel in the tank we were now using, I calculated that we did not have the minimum of extra fuel that is needed to fly to an alternative airport if we had a problem going into Mexico City. I could no longer count on the fuel remaining in the original tank. In addition, I could see rain showers ahead in the distant path. Since we would be approaching Mexico City through a mountain pass, I decided we would be wise to land and refuel before making the remainder of the trip to our final destination.

We had been flying outbound from a VOR (a type of aviation radio navigation facility) and would intersect an NDB from which we would next fly outbound to intersect an airway into Mexico City. This meant that I would have to rely upon navigational aids providing much less location reliability than I was accustomed to having. With the imminent rain, reduced level of available fuel coupled with the lack of the more precise VOR, I decided we would land there at the town where the beacon was located. I reviewed my aeronautical charts several times, but could not find an airport there. As we approached the town, I assumed there would be at least a small landing strip which would provide a safe haven for a few hours until the weather cleared. After all, if there was a radio navigational aid (navaid), there must be a nearby airport of some kind. As we came to the navaid, the needle flipped around, indicating we had passed the radio beacon. I could see the small village below. I began looking around for the airstrip. After circling the town a few times, I came to the unambiguous conclusion that there was no airport there, only the radio beacon.

At that point, I was not a happy pilot. During your flight training you practice what are called emergency landings. You never believe you will need to make one, but you practice it over and over, selecting where you will put the aircraft down, slowing the airspeed down, and assessing the wind direction from the movement of the trees. There were no trees. I selected the most straight road I could find and decided that would be where I would land the aircraft. After all, we have all seen such incidents on television. Years earlier, I had the thrill of a landing and take off from a small airport with a grass runway in Montana. I knew I could do it. I lined up the plane perfectly for the landing. We did a very slow decent. I held the nose of the aircraft high, which is the procedure for a soft field landing (one that is not on a paved runway). I heaved a great sigh of relief when then the main landing gear touched down normally, and we were rolling out down the road. I killed the engine immediately and even had the awareness to get the prop into a horizontal position, just in case we faced some additional problem.

As I was rolling along, the plane began to lose speed, and I slowly lowered the nose gear thinking we were done at last—at least for the moment. Then, suddenly the nose gear hit a pot hole on the dirt road, and it snapped off. It does not take a rocket scientist to know this is really bad news. In about two seconds the main gear collapsed, and the plane began skidding on the road. One of the wings clipped a maguey plant, and the aircraft spun to the left and came to an immediate halt. Within a single second, we exited the aircraft and all three of us were standing beside it assessing the damage. The fuselage and the tail of the aircraft looked undamaged. At least we were all safely on the ground.

Within sixty seconds approximately twenty locals descended upon us, all talking really fast. I began to speak with one of them in Spanish, and then mercifully, two American Mennonite missionaries pulled up in their car. They made certain we were safe. We removed our personal belongings from the plane, and they took us to their home.

They lived very humbly by any American standard. One of their tasks was to teach people how to construct and maintain outhouse toilets. This was not a rich area. The couple cooked their meals in an electric skillet and unlike many of the townspeople, they had glass in their windows and a concrete floor in their two room home. They were incredibly gracious to us. They fed us and drove us into the town, where I tried to make phone calls back to the States. It took quite a while to get a connection, but I finally reached someone and told them what had happened. I decided we needed to get to Mexico City to discern what to do next. The missionaries advised me to provide a generous *propina* (tip) to a local person who would guard the plane for a day or two, until I could get back.

We purchased bus tickets and rode about forty miles into Mexico City. I will never forget the little *Mexicano* boy who peered back over the seat in front of me and asked, *"¿De dónde es usted?"* (Where are you from?) We had a nice chat in his primary language and my secondary, but not particularly comfortable, language. Arriving in the big city, we went to our hotel and checked in. I then went straight to the American Embassy. When I arrived there, U.S. Marines were guarding the entrance. Once inside, I learned the vast majority of employees there seemed to be Mexicans, not Americans. That discovery was a big surprise. A representative there contacted someone at *Dirección General de Aeronáutica Civil* (the Mexican equivalent agency of our Federal Aviation Administration) on my behalf. He arranged a meeting for me to let them know what had happened.

I went to their offices and met with one of the *jefes* (bosses). He took my detailed statement in English. Someone then translated it to Spanish. I had to sign both copies verifying what I stated was true. The next morning the investigator took me to the plane for him to examine it. It was a very foggy day. Riding in the back seat of his car was more scary than landing my plane had been. He was zooming along at a speed that far exceeded my comfort level. On this superhighway, no one seemed to observe the regulation to drive in a particular lane. On the eastern edge of Mexico City, we came upon a huge pileup of over one hundred cars. They had crashed, due to lack of visibility. That blindness did not seem to impair the driver of our car. We arrived in the small town and located the plane. We got out, and he looked around and pulled out his notebook. He wrote down the serial number of the prop on the plane, made a few notes, and in about twenty minutes, we were headed back to Mexico City.

The investigator dropped me off at my hotel. This was my final time with the federal representative. He kept assuring me that I had no problem in Mexico. He was cordial but overly optimistic. I returned to the aircraft a few days later with a representative from the company that owned my rented plane. He handled all matters regarding the plane. I then returned to the city, having invested a great deal of time and energy on something that was not at all on my itinerary. However, the balance of my week there in the city was filled with exciting discoveries of things I had only read about. It was my first real experience using my remedial Spanish, moving around the city, interacting with their subway system, restaurants, the hotel desk clerks, and shopping.

If you thought that I could not have any additional growth opportunities on the trip after what I had already gone through, you would be wrong. My friends and I now needed to purchase one-way airline tickets to go back home to the States. I was thrilled to discover that Mexicana Airlines had a direct flight from Mexico City to Denver, with only one short stopover in Mazatlan. At the end of our stay, we boarded this flight at the Mexico City Airport. The flight was uneventful until we landed in Mazatlan. It was the hardest landing (say hit) on any runway that I have ever experienced, both in all my airline flying and even my beginning flight lessons. We hit so hard, I thought the landing gear would surely not survive the landing. There were gasps all around me, but I kept my cool. The pilot taxied up to the terminal as if everything was normal. Nothing about the memorable landing was ever said by the flight crew over the public address system upon arrival. The pilot remained in the cockpit with the door closed until all the passengers were deplaned. My friends and I landed safely back in Denver on schedule with absolutely no additional excitement except for our enthusiasm of being home once again.

My take-aways from this experience are endless. First of all, I appreciated my great private and commercial flight training, which prepared me to respond safely to this trauma in Mexico. I am appreciative of the wonderful hospitality I experienced both in the small town by the missionaries, but also by the local people who were so courteous to me while I waited hours for the intercity bus to arrive. The hotel staff in Mexico City was always courteous and seemed to appreciate my meager attempts to speak their language. I was appreciative of the U.S. Marines who were my welcoming committee at the Embassy, although they did not talk much at all. They were quite serious about their mission of guarding the Embassy. The staff there and at the Mexican aviation authority could have not been more courteous to this gringo.

As I look back, I still get a rush thinking about all these events. Fortunately, everything turned out well for me and my friends. We all had a life experience that could normally be found only in the movies. I know practicing patience through all these unfamiliar events kept me calm.

Local Transportation

Mass Transit

Many cities have mass transit systems. It is generally safer to travel with someone else than alone. You will have more eyes to keep you alert of your surroundings. Sometimes subways are safe and an excellent means of transportation. The fare to ride them is generally quite inexpensive. City buses can be confusing and sometimes quite unsafe. I avoid them all together. However, to travel between most cities you will have to rely upon busses. Inter-city buses sometimes have two classes of service, normally on separate buses. If at all possible, avoid the economy class. You could literally be traveling with chickens on top of the bus. I have. They will stop at every small pueblo on your route. They will almost certainly not be air conditioned. The express buses will be small "greyhound" type buses with reserved seating. They carry only sixteen to twenty passengers, a rest room, and sometimes even a snack counter and televisions on which they run movies. On these express buses, it is common to sell out of a particular departure time. Reservations and ticket purchases must sometimes be made in person rather than over the telephone. Do not expect to use a credit card for your ticket purchases. They will likely want cash.

Some of my most vivid memories of public transportation are from riding the Mexico City subway. One can travel all around metropolitan Mexico City for one very cheap fare. It was fascinating to discover that during rush hours some train cars are only for women. Men ride in separate cars. The signs on the subway improved my vocabulary. The words by the emergency stop switch warned never to pull this except in an emergency. The word used was *castigar*. That infinitive was not one I had ever learned in a Spanish class, but I was intuitive enough to know what it meant. I needed no part of castigation (punishment.)

Taxis

Most quality hotels will have a taxi stand or offer to call a legitimate taxi for you. A randomly selected taxi may bring you a driver that will greatly overcharge you or worse yet have criminal intentions. Always ask your hotel about passenger security and what a reasonable fare would be for a particular trip. Desk clerks can be relied upon to give accurate information. You are well advised to ask your hotel to schedule a known taxi driver to pick you up at a certain time. Hailing a taxi at random, especially when you are alone, is quite risky. In some cities, you ought not take a taxi that is not bonded through the hotel where you are staying. Inquire at the hotel desk about this safety issue.

Most taxis have no fare meters. Always discuss the charge with the driver before entering the taxi. Once inside, you have no power for negotiation. Fares are often set by law—laws you do not know, and fares you will not know. Have the fare in exact cash. Never expect the driver to make change. They seem to never have any change. Receipts might be available from the driver, but only if you ask. Plan ahead.

Driving

Before you leave home, make certain your driver's license has not expired. From personal experience, I know that you will not be able to rent a car if it has. There was a time when an international driver's license was needed, but I have not needed such a license anywhere in many years. Always be certain you have your valid current driver's license with you. Virtually no domestic auto insurance is valid in other countries. Many car rental companies ask you to purchase local auto insurance coverage. When I rent a car outside the United States, I make a point to always purchase the insurance, since my own car insurance is not valid in Mexico or many of other Latin American countries. The insurance is cheap compared to the trouble you will have without it. If you are in an accident, expect to pay cash for any repairs necessary. Like here, if the car is out of service due to your accident, even if it was not your fault, you might be charged a handsome daily fee for lost revenue until the car is repaired and back in service. You will have no control over these circumstances or time-frame. If you purchase their insurance, you avoid the entire problem. Never take a chance on this.

Always comply with the local requirements. Obey the traffic signals, even though many others may not. Do not speed, even though everyone around you will. Traffic accidents in Latin America can have serious legal consequences, especially if there are any questions about not having the proper paperwork. The concept of "innocent until proven guilty" is not embraced as universally as it is in the United States.

The cost of gas for your rental car might surprise you. It can be five to ten dollars per gallon in some places. Many countries have a nationalized oil company so there is no competition, and there is complete government control of prices. Monopolies provide no helpful price competition.

Traffic laws in Latin America are quite similar to those in the United States. They drive on the right side of the road. The traffic signs will be similar in shape, except the instruction displayed on the sign will be in Spanish. A stop sign in Mexico will display *Alto*. Other countries might display *Pare*. Street numbers and street signs will not have the systematic organization you will find in much of the United States. Sometimes street names are displayed on building walls at intersections. A GPS receiver with updated maps can be a great help. Plan ahead. Patience is a virtue.

Like all new adventures, driving in a foreign country can bring a few moments of emotional euphoria. It will likely cause you to be even more cautious than you would be at home. There is certainly nothing wrong with a little extra caution.

Part 3
We All Have the Same Needs

Language and Etiquette

One of the strongest positive impressions you can make on anyone when you visit their country is to speak their native language. The better your Spanish, the more personable the nationals will be toward you. You might mistakenly think Spanish is Spanish. Recall the English spoken by British people is considerably different from English spoken in Georgia or Texas. It would take a lifetime to know all the various accents and vocabulary throughout Latin America. I will never forget a local telecom engineer in my trade show booth at Caracas. He told me, "You are not speaking Spanish; you are speaking Mexican." Venezuelans and residents of many other South American countries speak a brand of Spanish called Castilian, which has a distinctive pronunciation of some words. People in Spain believe their Castilian is the authentic Spanish in the same way that Brits view their "accent" as the authentic English. Even though spoken Spanish varies, if you learn to speak proper Spanish from any region, you will be understood wherever you travel in Latin America (except perhaps in Brazil, where they speak Portuguese). Should you stay long or want to conduct business there, learning more of the language is critical.

Dialects will vary from country to country. In Venezuela the final "s" in many words is not pronounced—*ma(s)* not *mas* and *gracia(s)* not *gracias*. Of course, it is included if written. Also there is an influence from other European languages especially Portuguese (from Brazil) and Italian. Telephone conversations in Mexico are answered with *"¿Bueno?"* and ended with *"Adiós."* In Venezuela they are answered with *"(H)allo"* with a silent "h"and ended with *"Chow."*

There are many ways to begin learning Spanish. Online courses and phone apps, such as Rosetta Stone, Babble, and Berlitz, are great places to start. Select one of them and learn some of the basics, even if you will be a tourist for only a few days. Attending a Spanish language school will move you ahead more quickly. Almost all community colleges and universities offer courses that will last several months. Even Spanish language television channels are helpful learning tools. Asking where the *servicios* (rest rooms) are and politely greeting strangers is easy and important. Moving upward to dining out and ordering food and beverages will likely be the next tier of learning. The more Spanish you speak, the more you will enjoy your visit.

Regardless of how much you learn in academia, your first trip to Latin America will probably advance your language education beyond anything you will learn in a classroom. You will have the opportunity to learn with every waking minute. Learn from road signs, taxi drivers, hotel desk clerks, hotel maids, waiters, merchants in the marketplace, local television, and advertising as well as those with whom you will be doing business. Even your most feeble attempts to communicate in Spanish will usually precipitate a very warm and encouraging response. People will very likely help you with the gender and conjugation of each word, especially if you ask for their help.

I find the short laminated "Spanish for Dummies" brochure published by Wiley to be an easy review. After learning a small but useful vocabulary, I recommend a book I found particularly helpful: *Breaking Out of Beginner's Spanish* by Joseph J. Keenan. This is a goldmine. Small electronic translators also can be a great help. They are smaller than a pocket electronic calculator. You will never know all the vocabulary you encounter. There are also phone apps that provide quality translation. What is particularly nice is these options translate both directions. You can see a sign, enter the Spanish words from the sign, and translate what it means to English.

There are a number meanings for Spanish words that differ from what similar-sounding English words mean. For example, while *embarazada* sounds like the English word embarrass, it actually means pregnant. In Latin America, a taxi might be *disponible* (free or available), but it will not be *gratis* (free or at no charge). *Disfrutar* has nothing to do with fruit. It means to enjoy. But, be careful, you might not intend the nuance of a literal translation of *disfrútense*, which literally translated would be "Have fun with yourself." A much better choice would be to say *diviértanse*. English contains many homographs, words that are spelled and pronounced exactly the same, but that have multiple and unrelated meanings. For example we might use the word hard to say both hard disk and hard problem, but in Spanish we would say *disco duro* and *difícil problema*. Plan ahead to learn some of the basic vocabulary of the Spanish language before you set foot into Latin America.

Learn the language. Value the culture. Learn the geography and history. Travel books and maps from automobile clubs and on-line encyclopedias are excellent resources. Learn about the government structure, unusual laws—all countries have them. By no means travel to a country where you do not know the capital, name of the chief government administrator, and the phone number of the U.S. embassy. Most Latinos with small businesses will always be polite, but not always inclined do business with you unless they like you. They strongly prefer to do business with their friends. Small talk about their country is often important before moving to business, and this conversation is best done in their language.

One thing that might take getting used to is that Latin Americans want less physical space between you and them when they are talking to you. Expect them to stand a little closer to you in their discussions—especially if they are engaged with you or your products. They may often be twenty-four inches away from your face, rather than the three or more feet that is common in the United States. Do not back away from them as they talk to you. Stand there and let them take the initiative as to how close they will stand and sit when you are talking with them. They will also probably be much more vocally expressive than you are used to, especially if they are over forty years old. Many younger Latinos are more reserved, like people in the United States.

Another peculiarity you might notice is many elevators have a button for PB. This stands for *planta baja*. A literal translation for this would be lower level. In many countries this will be what Americans consider as the first floor or street level. A one on the elevator will take you to the first floor, which is actually the first floor above the street level, or what to us would be the second floor, unless of course there is an *entresuelo* (mezzanine) in which the first floor is actually the third floor. You will see this in hotels, shopping malls, and offices. Although it is rare, you should not be shocked to have the elevator door open and see an operator inside who will push the button for you. She might sit on a short stool as well as have a phone that might ring three or four times before she answers it.

Observe and learn from your own encounters as you travel. Strive to withhold negative judgments about ways that are dissimilar from those you know at home. Tolerance and patience here will be virtues. We will learn much more from someone who is a little different from us than someone who is just like we are.

Money

In areas where there is a great deal of tourist traffic, you might well be able to pay for your purchases in U.S. dollars. However, I recommend always having the equivalent of $150-$300 USD in local currency when you arrive at your destination. Learn the names, value, and denominations of their local currency. Foreign currency can probably be purchased at your bank or at your departure airport in the States. Should you have a late arrival, local currency exchange houses could be closed at your destination airport. You might need to take a taxi to your hotel, purchase a beverage, or provide tips for local assistance on some matter. Generally, the best rate of exchange for local currency is obtained in the country you are visiting. Remember, all currency exchange operations will make profit from your exchange transactions, both when you buy and when you sell currency. If you are outside the United States and are exchanging more than a few hundred U.S. dollars at a *casa de cambio* (currency exchange house), it is common to be asked to show your passport before the exchange will be authorized. Most hotels can also sell you local currency for U.S. dollars. However, the exchange rate is generally not as good as a *casa de cambio*. Be aware hotels will not usually sell back U.S. dollars in exchange for local currency.

Always notify your bank and credit card companies before you travel outside the United States. Give them specific dates and locations where you anticipate using your cards. If you fail to do this, you will often have your card deactivated by the institution because of possible fraud. They might call your home or office phone if that is the number in your account record and alert you. A voice mail left there will do you no good, if you are out of the country. It would be smart to verify that your credit card companies have your best contact phone number in your file.

Within large cities, you can find automated teller machines (ATMs). Some of these will permit local currency withdrawals from your U.S. bank account. Do not presume one will always work for you, just because it has a Bank of America or Cirrus sign on it. If you need cash, give it a try. Know that, as in the United States, you will be expected to use your pin (personal identification number) when using the card at an ATM. Expect a reasonable, but not great, rate of exchange. There will also be an additional fee added to your transaction cost for the use of the local ATM. Should the ATM malfunction, you take a risk of losing your card. It is always wise to have an additional card, just in case the ATM does not return your card. Also, be certain to notify your U.S. bank immediately if this happens, to prevent possible abuse of your card. Use caution when you draw cash from the machine, particularly if you are surrounded by people. Video security and good lighting around ATMs are not as prevalent in Latin America as in the United States. Recovery of any losses will be virtually impossible.

If you intend to use your credit card at local merchants, verify that the card company is giving you a reasonable exchange rate and expect an additional transaction fee because the transaction will not be in U.S. dollars. You can find this out by contacting the card companies before leaving home. Also, be certain to know the world-wide telephone number for the card so that you can contact them directly, if you have any problem with the card while you are abroad. Have the phone number written down somewhere other than on the back of the card. Plan ahead.

When you check into a hotel, never use your ATM card. Only use a credit card. The hotel will freeze credit on your card for the amount that they anticipate charging you for your bill. If you use a credit card, it only lowers your available credit by that amount. If you use an ATM bank card, they can freeze that amount of cash from your checking account. This means that pending transactions in your checking account can be impacted even though you have not yet paid your hotel bill. (This practice is also true in the United States.)

Place your return airline tickets, schedule, and the bulk of your cash in a hotel safe deposit box. These safes are generally quite secure and available to guests twenty-four hours a day. Never carry all the money that is on your person in your wallet. Only place the minimum cash that you might need to buy what you want and perhaps one credit card in your wallet. When you take your wallet out to buy subway tickets or pay in the restaurant, it is not smart to have a centimeter stack of cash bills in your wallet for all around you to see and be tempted to relieve you from it. I suggest that you keep your wallet in a front pants pocket rather than a hip pocket or purse. I have seen a pickpocket bump into someone and remove the wallet from a hip pocket without the owner even knowing it. If a thief wants to steal your purse, he will not be deterred by a your holding a strong leather strap attached to it. Many travelers use fanny packs for their cash, credit cards, and passports. Your access to these hidden items should be only when you are alone in places such as a restroom.

Dining

The cuisine of Mexico, Costa Rica, Cuba, Puerto Rico, and South American countries will vary by what and how they prepare their foods. Native Latin American cuisine in no way resembles the "Mexican food" widely consumed in the United States. Not everything is laced with steaming cheddar cheese and shredded lettuce. Most Latinos have never heard of sopapillas. Their primary meats are pork, beef, and chicken. Only on the coastal areas will you find an abundance of seafood. They eat many of the same foods that we do here, but they prepare them quite differently. You might find an option for a chocolate topping on your steak *(mole)*. If you like ice cream, you will probably love fried ice cream.

Restaurants typically do not remain open for meals throughout the day. Many only serve breakfast from seven until eleven in the morning. It is often quite hearty by U.S. standards with a choice of one to three meats, eggs, potatoes, toast, juice, and tea or coffee. Lunch will be served between one and five p.m. Dinner will be available between six and eleven in the evening. Between eleven and one p.m. and between five and six p.m. often there will be no service available. If you want to eat during these hours, the manager will politely tell you that they are closed now, and will reopen at the appointed time. He will also express his hope that you come back when they are open. There will be no feeling of regret that they cannot serve you when you wish, rather it is an invitation for you to return to eat at the prescribed hours. If it is inconvenient or impossible for you today, at least you will know their schedule so that tomorrow you can plan your day to dine at their restaurant.

All the rumors about careful eating are true. Never drink the local tap water. Drinking water is not the only risk. Anything that has been washed with tap water such as lettuce, tomatoes, and many other beautiful uncooked foods may contain undesirable bacteria. Bottled water and bottled and canned sodas are safe, if you know that the seals are not broken. If the seal is broken, do not drink it. Some economy-minded restaurateur could have refilled the container. If you use ice, make certain that it has been made with *agua purificado* (purified water). Almost anything cooked will be safe, whether vegetable or meat. Fruit is excellent, but you should be aware that you could become sick if the fruit was washed with water that is not purified. Fresh fruit that you personally peel, such as bananas, melon, or peaches is generally quite safe to eat. A little restraint with your food and beverages can save a lot of delay and discomfort should you get sick. Remember, not everyone cooks ice cream before freezing it. Brush your teeth only with bottled water.

When you have finished your meal, do not wait for the server to deliver your *cuenta*. Spanish uses the more correct word bill *(cuenta)* rather than the peculiar word used in the States—check. I have never been given a check from the restaurant owner after completing my meal there. In the United States we highly value rapid service. The Latino waiter wants you to relax and certainly does not want to add stress to your dining experience by bringing you the bill prematurely. He would consider it impolite to present a bill without having been asked for it. They do not want to rush you. That action would imply that it is now time for you to depart. When you are ready for the bill, ask for it.

Many restaurants add what they say is a 10% service charge to your bill. This is not a tip in the strict sense. It will not go to your waiter. Many restaurants charge and collect this and then ostensibly distribute it back to some of their employees - and not necessarily in an equitable manner. This income for those employees typically becomes a part of their regular income—an increase from their typically low wages. If you have a better than a regular level of service, and want to reward your server, just add in a *propina* (tip) when you pay the bill, just as you would in the States. Be aware that Americans often pay a larger than expected tip. A waiter who provides exceptionally good service in Latin America expects a 10% to 15% tip, not 20% or 25% as in the United States.

Always expect to conduct your payment in local currency. If you expect to receive change back from the restaurant, expect that it will be in the local currency, not U.S. dollars, even if they are gracious enough to receive U.S. dollars in payment. You are a guest in their country.

Attire

I recommend that you not wear expensive jewelry if you will be roaming the cities. If you are in remote areas, there is no need to try to impress anyone. Nice rings, watches, and flashy jewels will draw public attention to yourself. Such displays can invite unnecessary risk for these items being stolen from you. Pickpockets are more common in some countries than at home.

Modest dress should be the norm for the traveler, except in resort areas, where leisurewear and swim suits are often the norm. Do not walk through cathedrals with shorts and t-shirts. Respect what they respect. You are a guest in their country. Plan ahead.

The standards for business attire in Latin America are similar to the U.S., though just a little more formal. In most offices ladies may be wearing suits and high heel shoes. Professional men nearly always wear dark suits, white shirts, and ties. Colored shirts are virtually never seen in the business world, but are common in social gatherings. Many people will judge your level of education based on your choice of attire. They will judge your character by your behavior.

Shopping

While large American-based super stores are being introduced into large cities in Latin America, much of your shopping will likely be in small specialty stores. In Latin America, the large super stores operate very much like they do here. However, buying procedures are often different in small stores. There, after you have selected the items you want, you do not always carry them to the cash register. The clerk might write out an invoice in longhand and give it to you, and then set aside your purchased good. You then take the invoice to the *caja* (literally box, but here it means cash box or cashier) to pay the invoice. After you have paid, the clerk will deliver your merchandise to the exit door for you to pickup as you leave.

It is still common to find that some stores and even government offices observe siesta hours. This can mean that they are closed from eleven in the morning until two or three p.m. at which time they reopen and remain open until eight or nine in the evening. In those places where the siesta is observed, you might feel inconvenienced. The people working there probably do not feel that way. They enjoy the mid-day break. Plan ahead. Patience is a virtue.

The historic practice of bargaining back and forth for merchandise that you wish to purchase is virtually non-existent except in the areas heavily visited by tourists. The practice of negotiating is common especially where cruise ships dock and send their travelers into the marketplace to secure their bargain purchases to take home. For example, in Cozumel, Mexico, as soon as you exit your ship, the docks lead you to ample shopping including the "Myan Flea Market." A few blocks from this you find the *"Marcado Municipal."* Both only accept cash and it is not unusual to be able to negotiate pricing.

Virtually no one will accept your check for payment. Some will accept certain credit cards, but many businesses will not accept any credit cards. The merchant fees charged in some countries are so high that many stores choose not to offer this convenience. (It is common for these fees to be three to five times the fees paid in the United States.)

Major hotels and large restaurants will accept credit cards. If you wish to use credit cards there, be certain to take several different cards with you. Know your credit limit on each account. Your primary card may be declined for authorization, even though there may be no legitimate grounds. The clerk will not call the United States to check on a possible mistake. He receives his authorization from his local bank system. Have one or two other cards to relieve your stress in this situation. Know the out of country phone numbers for customer service for each card, in the event you need to resolve a problem while abroad.

All stores will accept local currency. In resort communities, United States dollars may be accepted. However, you will probably pay more with dollars than with local currency. Some stores in Mexico list both *pesos* and *dólares americanos* (US dollars), and you can notice that they will not always update their pricing based on the current exchange rate.

Most importantly, prepare and enjoy your shopping experiences. Latin America has some of the most amazing artwork and jewelry. Larger stores may even ship items back to the States for you. Remember, some items cannot be carried onto the plane and that some items legally purchased abroad cannot be brought into the United States. One friend purchased a blowfish that was dried and arranged into a piece of artwork. This item was not permitted and taken away by U.S. customs at the port of entry. Had she been aware of the rules and guidelines on custom restrictions of the State Department (www.travel.state.gov), she would have not purchased the artwork.

Sightseeing

Every country will present great opportunities to learn about the local life. Always check for local information on historical, cultural, and scenic learning opportunities. Whenever I travel to an area where I do not have much familiarity, I try to take in some of the local culture and visit places that are important to those who live there. You can certainly do some of this research before leaving home. As you search on Google, Yelp, Trip Advisor, and others, look for information on the country and cities you plan to visit. Learn about the history, government, geography, major industries, important monuments, museums, and preferred tourist attractions. Your hotel staff can often provide you some suggestions once you arrive. Hotels often have racks of promotional literature about things to do in the area. You might find musical performances, local bands, and parks that mark important events in their history. Verify the hours of being open to visitors. Some municipal parks are closed at nighttime. Many museums are closed on Monday. Sometimes, they might not have continuous hours during the day. Be intentional. Plan ahead and check.

Strolling through the large, beautiful Chapultepec Park in Mexico City one warm afternoon, I was thirsty and came upon a small stand that was selling *refrescos* (soda pop). I ordered a Coca Cola and the clerk pulled out a bottle which he had on the shelf, and popped the cap off and handed it to me. It was my first experience of drinking a Coke *caliente*. While that word literally means hot, in this context it means at room temperature. Ice is often not available. I so much prefer having ice with in my Cokes! This was simply one more growth opportunity for me. Value the opportunity to discover and see new experiences while you travel.

Telephone Service

Learn quickly how to use the local telephone service. Virtually no country in Latin America has any technology history that will be comparable to the United States. Fortunately, the advent of cellular technology over the past thirty years has bypassed the need to rely on traditional telecommunication technology. Many areas now use cellular phones almost exclusively because no reliable wireline infrastructure exists.

Before you leave the States, find out the country and city code where you will be traveling. Find your hotel telephone number. Never trust anyone to give you reliable information about the local phone system. Before you leave, call the hotel directly to confirm that the number is correct. Save the number in your phone. Ask them for an alternate telephone number. I recommend getting the email address for the front desk of the hotel as well. Only in the largest cities in Latin America will it be commonplace to have one main telephone number with many lines that connect to that number. It is common for a company to have three or four different telephone numbers. If the number that you call is busy, you must hang up and call another number. Calls do not necessarily roll over to the unoccupied telephone lines automatically as they do here.

Plan ahead for your calls back to the States. If you call home from your hotel room phone, you may have to ask the hotel operator to place a call back to the States. Expect to hang up and wait for the operator to call you back in fifteen to twenty minutes when he has an open line and can place your call. Long distance calls charged to your hotel room will usually be 300% to 1000% of the actual cost of the telephone call. Inquire at the hotel desk about the charges before you make the calls so you will know exactly what to expect. It is also common to have a ten to fifteen dollar fee to connect you to an American long-distance operator so you can use your calling card.

If you plan to take your cellular phone, call your local carrier before leaving home to find out if the destination permits roaming. Many do. Even if they tell you no, it is entirely possible that service may actually be provided. Many international cellular carriers have cross related roaming agreements, which will permit easy automatic roaming access. Sometimes local access requires the use of a credit card for activation. Verify with your cellular carrier that your phone is compatible with the cell phone system where you will be. Some inexpensive phones will not work outside of the United States. The establishment of these services can usually be taken care of before you leave the states to permit full cellular telephone use upon arrival. Find out the per minute charge from that country to home. Avoid a surprise with local talk and data charges. You might be unpleasantly surprised. It can be as high as one to three dollars per minute. Also, there is virtually no privacy on cellular telephone service. Anyone can monitor most cellular telephone calls with a specially equipped radio receiver, if that is their intention.

Local pay telephone service is seldom accessible with coins. Almost all countries require use of locally purchased telephone cards. These look like credit cards, but actually provide prepaid credit. They can usually be purchased in stores and at the check-in desks of most luxury hotels. When the card is inserted into the card reader in the phone, the display will report the amount of credit remaining on the card. When the credit is used up, you discard the card and buy a new one. Many toll free (800) numbers within the U.S. will probably not work from Latin America. Agreements now provide these services for companies that want this expanded coverage area for additional costs and using different toll-free numbers.

There is an emerging technology that can be particularly useful. Local car rental agencies and other operations can sometime rent you a portable device that will work throughout the country. It is called a hot spot. This will be a small box about the size of a package of cigarettes. It will have a rechargeable battery. This device will provide you with Wi-Fi service wherever you go. Where it is available, get it. The rental might be thirty-five dollars for a week, but it will allow you to make Wi-Fi phone calls, web surfing, and video calls back to the United States via the Internet at no additional cost, if your phone can operate over Wi-Fi. Also, since many hotels offer Wi-Fi, using this for local calls or calls back home can be a wise choice. These options would be a great way to save money over using the local telephone networks.

Electricity

Throughout all of Latin America the electrical power will depend entirely in which country you are. Mexico and most of Central America will be 120 Volts 60 Hz, the same electrical power as in the States. Many countries of South America will be 240 volts and either 50 or 60 Hz. If your location has 240 volts, it can be easily converted to the voltage we use here in the States. Many appliances you might take will work fine on 240 volts. Check the specifications on the device. Often, you can use your phone chargers and small electrical appliances without the need for transformers, if they accept voltage up to the local amount supplied. If your device will only accept 110 or 120 volts, you will always need one of the small inexpensive voltage converter appliances with you. No matter what local voltage is supplied, a variety of outlet types can require an array of plug adapters. These are readily available in the United States from many department stores and on-line. They are also available at most destination airport shops, but the purchase price will likely be higher than at home. Be prepared and plan ahead.

When 110-120 volts is supposed to be the norm, do not be surprised if the actual level of voltage is lower. Levels of 100 volts are considered acceptable at many locations. The voltage can also vary throughout the day. Ground fault protection circuits (GFI—the outlet that trips and turns off the outlet, if too much current is drawn) required here in bath rooms and kitchens are nonexistent in Latin America. Three prong (grounded) outlets will not usually be available except in the newest of construction. For that reason, you should always have several ground cheaters (the type of plug that accepts a three prong plug but will plug into the older two prong outlet) to be used with your electrical equipment. They are available in all local hardware stores in the United States. It is also a good idea to always take an power strip with surge protection, if you need to operate multiple devices at the same time.

Healthcare

Travel with me for a moment to the beautiful colonial city of Morelia, Michoacán, Mexico. It was founded in the early 1500s by the Spanish. One Saturday morning, I proceeded to the office to work with my local software sales representative. I had a strong thirst early in the day, and consequently I drank a lot of water. By ten o'clock in the morning, I had visited the men's room five or six times. I took a break and laid down on the office sofa for approximately thirty minutes. Eventually, I told my friend that I needed him to take me back to my hotel. I felt sick. I felt quite sick. I laid down on my bed in the hotel room and turned on the television. After watching it for an hour, I was so sick, I did not have the energy to get up and change the television channels. A gringo plight that I had heard about for years had become my reality. I had no hunger for the next thirty-six hours. Fortunately, I had prepared in advance for this possibility by bringing suitable medicine with me. I started taking it immediately. After two days, I enjoyed my first food intake - two pieces of dry toast. During the time in my room, I was completely disinterested in reading, conversation, or anything that was even slightly engaging. In these circumstances, Latinos sometimes recommend transitioning back to life with a Coke and a twist of lime. It was truly magnificent after *Moctezuma* left town.

If you are rigorously careful with your food and beverage consumption, you probably will have no difficulty with stomach or intestinal problems. It is wise to buy any anticipated medications before you leave home. By all means, discuss with your doctor what you should do, if you are taken ill on your travels in a foreign country. I always travel with an inexpensive antibiotic and over the counter antacid tablets. Upon the first sign of an uneasy stomach, I immediately start both medications. Continue to force yourself to drink purified water to prevent dehydration. Remember to never brush your teeth with tap water. Keep your mouth closed when showering. While many luxury hotels have their own water purification system, rely upon it at your own risk. Please inquire if the hotel operates such a system. Smaller locally owned hotels may have running or hot water only during certain hours of the day.

Should you require medical attention, there are medical doctors, hospitals and pharmacies in all of the major cities throughout Latin America. Your hotel desk can probably refer you to a qualified medical facility to help you if needed. Depending upon where you are, the level of care might be the same as available in the United States. However, medical care in some locations might feel you are in a third world country. When I had to visit an emergency room in a large city in Puerto Rico, I was shocked to see the hallway walls on both sides lined with gurneys and people sitting on them in lines waiting to see an emergency room doctor. Many medical facilities will have someone who speaks English to help you, but speaking the local language will be of immense help. Knowing the Spanish words for parts of your body will certainly be helpful as well.

It is likely that no one outside of the United States will take your medical insurance. Check on this before you leave if you have private medical insurance. Plan ahead. You might have to pay with cash. Most Medicare policies will not cover you out of the country. In some instances, after you have paid your medical expense and return home, you can file for some level of reimbursement, but if you receive any, it will not be much.

When you travel abroad, I strongly recommend that you purchase a travel insurance policy that will cover any medical expenses while away. In the event of a major emergency, these policies will generally provide you an immediate return to your home city to receive medical treatment as part of their coverage. These can be purchased through auto clubs and other insurance organizations and certainly through your travel agent. It is relatively inexpensive, and if needed, it will be a great relief for you.

Police

It can be quite startling to see security guards and police carrying machine guns. This is very common, especially at airports, large public gatherings, banks, and government offices throughout Latin America. There seem to be a lot of policemen, especially in large cities. Perhaps they are intentionally conspicuous to serve as a deterrent to crime. I have never been tempted to stop and strike up a conversation with any of them. Some countries even have multiple police systems. Like here, there can be both Federal and State police in addition to local authorities. Each one will have a geographic and particular crime jurisdiction.

If you have an emergency and want to call the police from your cell phone, calling 911 will not always get you help. Its use is widespread through Mexico and more and more countries in Latin America. But, find out the emergency phone numbers for the countries where you will be traveling before you leave the United States. Search for this on Google for up-to-date details. There is no universal consistency, although in most countries it will be a three digit number. Often, there are different emergency numbers for different needs, such as police, ambulance, or fire. Also, do not count on the person who receives your call to speak English particularly well. Again, the more Spanish you speak, the more effective your phone call will be. Reject the entitlement mentality that you deserve that these public servants speak English. Plan ahead for this contingency. Patience is a virtue.

Business Holidays

Latinos celebrate many more holidays from work than we do in the United States. Since Latin America is predominately Roman Catholic, many religious holidays are also national holidays. Celebration of *El Día de los Muertos* (the Day of the Dead), Christmas, Lent, Good Friday, and Easter will always be observed. Each state within a country will have state holidays in addition to federal holidays. These days honor certain wars and important historical political and military figures. Many businesses will be closed on Sunday all day. In addition to holidays, during the last two weeks of December and the time around elections, commerce comes to a virtual standstill. When funding runs out for certain state and federal agencies, they close their offices, sometimes for days or weeks at a time. If you need a response from them for something, you will simply have to wait. There will be no alternative. Always plan ahead.

Holidays such as Mother's Day and Columbus Day are celebrated on the actual day of occurrence, rather than moved to Sundays or Mondays as observed in the United States. Each country celebrates a unique Independence Day. You will find no countries in Latin America or anywhere else that celebrate July 4th, our Independence Day. My first July 4th out of the United States seemed a bit strange. I attended a local parade commemorating a national military hero. There was no hint of our Independence Day. That moment clearly left me with a feeling of being really far away from home. They will not celebrate the birthdays of the many American presidents as we do in the States. Know that the United States is not the center of everyone's world, contrary to what many gringos think.

Part 4
Conducting Business in Latin America

Cultivating Business

If you intend to expand your business into Latin America, develop a strategic sales plan and support plan for your products and services. This can sometimes be best accomplished by working with a local professional who knows both the local culture and knows the necessary specialized technology concerning what you are offering. You might focus on a limited geographic area, or you might work on a particular sector of an industry. Selling in Latin America is very much like selling in the States. Either you motivate a new customer to come to you, or you go directly to prospective customers. For increased credibility, your major printed sales literature must be made available in Spanish as well as in English. You must also speak some Spanish or employ someone who can speak on your behalf.

The most common way to motivate a potential customer to approach you is by strategic use of Google. Google Analytics and Google AdWords are powerful forces to help drive people to your website. You will need to do research on the key words (both English and Spanish) that people use when searching for your products or services. Of course, you must provide a stellar website using great photos, with clear explanations of what you offer, what its benefits would be to use, who you are, and a very simple way for them to contact you through a web form collecting their email address and phone number. As you design your contact web form, you might wish to ask some pre-qualifying questions in order to find out how serious the person is. This is precisely the same approach if you were talking in person. Let your contact form help you pre-qualify your prospective customer, or better yet cue you that this person is not a likely customer. If your entire sites is not multi-lingual, it would be smart to have several pages dedicated to using Spanish. Online networking such as Facebook, Instagram, Linked-In, and Align are widely used throughout Latin America. Make your presence know there as well.

When you pursue prospective customers, you can sometime rent email lists of subscribers from a trade publication. Economical web-based emailing companies can help you with email promotions and the collection of the contact information. You can also approach some of your current customers and obtain referrals from them for you to contact. Also, as you identify the profile of your domestic customers, you probably can identify people in these foreign countries that have similar professional profiles. Sometimes you can access members of trade associations or professional associations whose specialized need you can fill. As with all sales prospecting, this requires an ongoing, significant initiative on your part.

Finally, I trust that you recognize that humor does not transfer to other cultures particularly well. I would refrain from trying to use humor in your personal or business encounters or sales literature. What might be quite funny to us here can be either perplexing or offensive in another culture, even though that might not be your intention.

Business Meetings

Expect to have your patience put to the test when you have a business meeting. Gringos generally live in anticipation of the future and are acutely conscious of time. We live, both at work and play, from detailed preplanned schedules and agendas. Many Latinos primarily live almost entirely in the present. Nothing is more important than what they are doing at the present moment. When you work with them, they are often totally focused on you and your conversation. Most business people will not allow interruptions to your meeting. They are being respectful of your time together. When you and they are through, they move to the next person. This will be true with the person before your appointment as well as the one after yours. For that reason, do not be surprised if your 10 a.m. appointment will not commence until 11:30 or 12:00. Meetings will require much more patience and personal engagement and courtesy than is typical in the United States. It is common to spend two to three times the length of time you might expect for the same type of meeting in the States. This same focus on the present moment also will be the norm for the hotel desk clerk and the waiter taking your order at a restaurant. Patience is a virtue.

Plan to arrive at your meeting destination early, because it will likely take time to pass through building security, which is common in many office buildings. Before you can enter an office building, you typically have to present identification such as your passport. You will have to disclose who you are visiting, where you intend to go in the building, and receive written permission to enter usually in the form of a pass. When you leave, you will return the building pass to the security officer. Some buildings will require you to leave some form of important personal identification with them to be picked up when you leave. Do not ever leave your passport or driver's license. Many times an official-looking photo identification card might be sufficient. Many residences also will be surrounded by high walls with only one or two secured entrances into the area. Expect to see more security in most of Latin American than we normally experience in the States.

Every important business person will have a gatekeeper. View this receptionist or secretary as a friend not an adversary. Build a bridge with the gatekeeper when you are in the office. When you arrive for your appointment, introduce yourself, give him or her your business card, and make a friendly comment or two. Advise the gatekeeper that you are expected and at what time your appointment is scheduled. After your appointment concludes, always go back to express thanks for the help that was provided. Take this opportunity to confirm the boss's phone number and email address. This will pay off strongly in the future, when you need access to her boss. She can often personally take a message to his desk or tell you when he will return, if she knows you. Such individual attention is almost never available to the complete stranger, no matter how important it is to you or how polite you may be over the phone. In Latin America, many employees are either afraid to or prohibited from calling or faxing long distance to the United States. They will not return your call unless they know who you are and also want to talk to you.

Every commercial exchange is also a social exchange. Personal relationships lay the foundation for almost all business relationships in Latin America. Do not expect to commence serious business discussions until you have spent some time discussing each other's families. While Latin American business persons are generally more personal than U.S. business persons, they are also often more formal. You will be expected to address your business acquaintances by title both in person and in correspondence. For example, you should say *Ingeniero* Camorlinga rather than *Señor* Camorlinga or *Licenciada* Moreno rather than *Señora* Moreno. Latinos typically have a first and middle name followed by their father's last name and then their mother's last name. You generally drop their mother' s name in conversation but always use it in formal writing. I recommend addressing all women regardless of their age as *señoritas* rather than *señoras* unless they tell you different.

Spanish has both a formal and a familiar presentation of the language. Always use the formal (*usted*, not *tú*) when addressing a business person or someone who considers himself in authority over other people. They might address you in the familiar, but stick to the formal until you are invited to greet them with the informal pronouns and verbs. This will be important throughout all of Latin America as well as with Spanish-speaking Americans.

Respect and courtesy will always be important in your business transactions. When you give personal respect to people, they will usually return the courtesy. If that does not happen, move on. Your counsel is not desired by them in business. You will not change them. Never let anyone's discourtesy to you dictate how you respond back to them. Manage your emotions well. Patience is a virtue.

Selection of an Attorney

If you do much business within a foreign country, you might need to have a working relationship with a attorney who is licensed there. Just as in the United States, working with a local competent law firm in the country can benefit you a great deal. He or she can acquaint you with many of the credit, intellectual property, tax, and employment laws of the country. They most certainly will be different from the laws in the United States. Many lawyers in foreign cities have an ongoing exchange relationship with large law firms here in the States. If your domestic law firm has no recommendations for referrals, contact the country's closest consulate in the United States or the American Embassy in that country. They often have personal knowledge about individual lawyers or at least will maintain a list of lawyers who have registered their request for referrals. In that case, do a thorough checkout of references. If possible, visit their offices and make your own evaluation.

It is especially helpful if your counsel understands both the laws and business culture in both countries. He or she should have a great deal of business acumen, especially if the attorney practices in both countries. Be certain you are crystal clear about the area of law in which you are seeking advice. Law has many specialties. Contract law is a special area, just as is intellectual property and civil litigation. Be focused on specifically what you want your attorney to do for you. It is much less stressful to identify with whom and how you will work together, before you have a critical need for their services. Plan ahead.

Contracts

If you are doing much business within Latin America, you will learn a lot about the laws of each country. There are many differences from laws and procedures here. Your contract should identify both parties and specify who is authorized to take action on the contract and the products and services which will follow. Anticipated time frames for the starting and ending of your contractual obligations are desirable. Just as in America, contracts are extremely beneficial to both parties when they are developed with mutual consent and authorized by people with integrity.

You will need to decide in what currency you will conduct your transactions. Major business are accustomed to buying in U.S. dollars. This policy will pass any instabilities of local currency value fluctuation to your customers. This variation will be perceived as a varying price for your products. For example, today your $100 (US) item might cost $2000 Mexican pesos. Tomorrow, this same $100 item might cost 2100 Mexican pesos due to an ever-changing currency exchange rate. You might wish to provide proposals in local currency and accept payment in it as well. If you do, make certain that the exchange rate you use is realistic. You would be assuming the risk of fluctuating currency values. Include an additional fee for your currency exchange and banking fees. Fees of $50 or more are typical. Bank wire transfers are common. You can secure the needed inbound international wire transfer details from your local bank. It will include the SWIFT code (bank identifier code). This process is only slightly more complicated that a domestic wire transfer. Expect that international wire transfers will take longer to execute than domestic ones.

If you are doing your actual business from within the United States, clearly state that you wish to avoid or minimize any income tax in the other country. If you have an office there, you can expect to be liable for taxes on any profit made in that country. For a small business this can be quite challenging. You must operate in accordance with their tax laws.

Even though you are doing business in the United States and simply selling to someone in another country, it is not unheard of for their government withhold the local income tax on the sale from payment to you. Bear in mind that such tax will be on the gross amount of the sale, not a tax related to your profit. If you can clarify that the full invoiced amount will be paid, you can avoid a terrible surprise. I have experienced Latin governments requiring the withholding of a portion of your sales price from the transfer and paying it directly to their government. It is certainly possible that they can tax your sale. As obnoxious as this might seem, should this happen you will not be able to persuade the company to pay your full invoiced amount. If you face this, you will probably need to attempt to claim a tax credit for foreign taxes paid against your United States federal tax to partially recover this loss. Please understand this is a foreign government income tax that is charged to you. It has no bearing on the importation and sales taxes your customer must also pay. If you qualify for a foreign tax credit on your domestic tax returns, you will not suffer the full loss. For more details contact your tax accountant.

In addition to addressing the amount and form of payment you will receive, you should identify when and where payment is due and penalties should the payment not be timely received, along with when and where your services or products will be delivered. If there are additional expenses such as shipping, travel costs, or promotion, the foreseeable expenses regarding these items should be specified.

Specify in what courts or by arbitration you both agree to settle disputes that might arise in the performance of the contract. A domestic lawsuit will probably be less expensive, but probably a foreign court in the country where your loss occurred might be more helpful in pursuing your collection. Business owners eventually learn that winning a judgment in court does not mean you will actually collect the award. Collection is usually a separate battle.

It is common to issue two editions of the final agreement in both English and Spanish. Both copies will be signed by both parties. Expect to specify which one will rule in the event of a dispute. There will never be an identical translation. While certain forms of electronic signatures are becoming quite common in the United States, be certain that this form of authorization is binding in other country by consulting with your attorney if you wish to use it. Often the old school policy of a handwritten signature is the only way to bind a contract.

By all means, enter into an international contract only after you have consulted with your local attorney who has thoroughly reviewed your proposed contract. While all attorneys want to write your contracts, I have found that the best-suited contracts for my business needs are drafted initially by the parities. Once you and the other party agree with the precise details, then have the attorneys for both parties review and make suggestions to be certain that no one is breaking the law. It is quite common to have several iterations back and forth before it is finalized. Even with all this caution, a written contract is not worth much if the parties are not operating with integrity. Legal remedies for curing a default on a contract are always costly. Remember even if you get a court judgment in your favor, receiving the judgment does not mean you will necessarily receive the payment without also initiating legal action for collection in the foreign jurisdiction.

Extending Credit

Just as every culture has honest, efficient, productive, liquid businesses, each culture also has the opposite. It is not wise to extend credit in greater amounts than the dollar amount you would willingly loan to your customers, for that is precisely what you would be doing. At times extending credit could be prudent and stimulate your sales, if you can afford to take the risk. Sometimes, terms actually make the sale. However, making the sale is a long way from having the money from the sale in the bank. The costs for collections of past due receivables or worse yet lawsuits to obtain judgments followed by subsequent collections will often far exceed the profit margins on a sale. It can easily cost $75,000 to get a modest foreign lawsuit underway, even before trial. Small businesses should avoid this problem entirely. Know your costs. Know your risks. Know when you must cut your losses.

The governments of most Latin American countries want to keep local money inside their country. For that reason, do a little research before you make large marketing investments. Build a strong case that you will have a worthy market. The actual cost for your customers to buy your foreign goods will exceed your sale price by at least shipping and local taxes. Many countries impose a tax of 10-35% for U.S. merchandise imported. Mexico has increased their national sales tax to 16%. Certain other countries charge up to 19% national sales tax. This tax is imposed on all merchandise purchased within the country. It will also likely be collected on all imported goods and will be in addition to any other taxes on imported products.

Your customer will always consider all these local taxes plus your selling price, when he decides whether or not to proceed with the purchase.

Some companies strictly impose a limit on the amount of U.S. dollars that an individual or company can purchase with their bank or credit cards. This limit can be as low as $2000 USD. Any significant sales to these individuals will have to be creatively structured. Medium and large businesses can usually assist you with solutions to this problem. You would do well to follow their suggestions, if you are comfortable with them. It is likely that they have repeatedly solved this problem in the past.

In Latin America, the original invoice from a vendor has much greater significance than it does in the States. Invoices are seldom sent via the mail. The typical billing and payment process is quite tedious. For example, in Mexico, for many years invoices had to be printed on preprinted numbered invoice forms. These forms had specific federal requirements and could be printed only by a few government authorized printers. Each of these forms would contain an area detailing the required federal registration of the company that issued the invoice. Computer generated invoices on blank paper were illegal in Mexico. Because of the significance of these invoices, once they were prepared by the seller, they were usually personally delivered to the purchaser by the seller. The buyer issued a receipt for the invoice. On the receipt there was often a date or time specified when the seller could return to receive a check in payment for the invoice. At the appointed time, the seller again returned to the buyer with the invoice receipt to accept the check for payment. Around 2010 the Mexican government, along with many other Latin American countries passed laws that now require e-Invoicing through a federally controlled system, requiring long-term data storage. When you make a sale be certain that your invoice will be considered valid by the persons authorized to pay.

In many small businesses in the United States it is a common policy to scan or make a photocopy of each check received before it is deposited. In some countries it is illegal to copy a check. Even where it may be legal, it will probably be perceived to be illegal. You should not expect professional photocopy services to accommodate your request, if you are in those countries. These details do not particularly affect a United States company who is simply selling to Latin American customers and invoicing under our laws. But, it is helpful to understand some of the business dynamics that your Latin American clients are accustomed to using. Many practices are substantially different from the way business is conducted at home.

If you begin to have collection issues from customers who reside out of the United States, I recommend you cease extending credit to them, until such time as they are current. It is good to not provide services or goods out of the country without a 100% prepay, if you can enforce that policy. You will probably not be able to do this with some government agencies. In those cases, you will need to make a business decision regarding the risk you are willing to take by extending credit to them.

More and more Latin American businesses are purchasing goods and services produced in the United States through procurement or trading companies that make the purchase on their behalf. Frankly, this can be a great assistance in the sale, if such an arrangement is in place. You sell directly to that company that already has a method of payment to United States companies in place. Often, you can then ship directly to the trading company located in the US, and they are then responsible for shipping and customs clearing and any required duty in the foreign country. But, be cautious dealing with them, so as to avoid all the same issues you might have dealing directly with the end customer in another country.

Trade Publications

If you wish to expand your business into Latin America, learn about the history, present environment, and future of your type of business there. Virtually every industry will have trade publications. Unlike consumer publications, a trade publication covers a specific topic or industry for the people who work in that industry. They usually provide many more industry-related details than would be of interest to the reader of consumer magazines. Some trade publications are operated by groups of manufacturers. Some are published by trade associations. Others are simply commercial publications that focus on media delivery to a certain profile of subscribers. Most trade publications contain a great deal of information about new technology that is emerging around the world. In virtually every industry, there will be valued trade publications read by people in that arena.

It is particularly important for you to obtain subscriptions to the same trade publications that are read by your potential customers. If you are unfamiliar with trade publications in the sectors where you have customers, contact your existing customers and find out on whom they rely for industry news. Also, do extensive Google searching on the types of products you sell. A great place to begin searching is with "trade publications for (insert your industry or product)." Examine the websites of your competitors. Attempt to find out where they spend their advertising dollars.

A number of international trade publications are published in English, but if you can obtain and study these trade publications in Spanish, you can gain an excellent technical vocabulary. This vocabulary will be practical and probably not available via Spanish video courses or from dictionaries. These same publications can also be an excellent forum for your regular company press releases and advertising. You can also learn about scheduled industry trade shows. Sometimes a well placed article in one of these publications can provide more responses than can paid advertising. For many industries, these international trade publications are edited and published by companies in the United States. When you contact the publishers, seek to identify the size of their circulation and a breakdown on the job titles for their subscribers.

There was a time when printed trade publications were what every publisher issued. The cost of editorial and magazine layout has gone up over the recent years. But, the cost of printing and local distribution in various countries has gone up dramatically. As a result, almost all trade publications now distribute via email. The magazines are laid out just as if they would be printed, but are viewed on a computer or phone. Some publishers still distribute printed copies.

Each publisher will have a website, which you should examine in detail. The publisher will provide details of their subscribers if you indicate an interest in advertising with them, but do not expect to see a BPA media audit, providing an independent third-party verification of ownership and circulation as was common a few years ago. You might also find that these publications will rent their subscriber email lists for a direct marketing campaign, if that is of interest to you.

Exhibiting at Trade Shows

If exhibiting at trade shows works well for you in the United States, perhaps you should consider trade shows for marketing your products and services in Latin America. As you research what shows are presented in a region, you may be surprised that you will have to make choices from several. Just has in the United States, it is critical to choose the preferred shows in which you exhibit. If the exposition has been conducted for several years, the show management should be able to provide you with a reliable profile of show attendees. This information can give you important input as to whether or not this would be a good show at which you might wish to exhibit. I suggest that you promote your participation in the trade show through a timely press release that either goes into your industry trade journals or at least an email to all your customers in that region and any pre-customers who have previously contacted you as well as on your website.

Many of the shows in Latin America are organized by companies based in the United States. There will be a floor plan distributed showing where you will place your exhibit and a brief description published about your products or services. It is quite common to be sold your booth space as a package that includes all the items that you typically have as an option when exhibiting at a show here. The package will normally include your carpet, signage, lighting, electricity, table, chairs, booth cleaning, and booth security.

If you elect to display your products or services at a trade show in Latin America, you will find the administrative arrangements there will be virtually identical to what you have here. The booth space you occupy will be rented using their contract. Just like the laws in Latin America, the trade show regulations and contracts can be somewhat flexible, largely depending upon your attitude. Sometimes official looking papers from you will help. Frequent use of corporate and professional seals will increase your perceived importance and credibility. You might choose to emboss your corporate seal over your signature on the contract. This will probably feel strange to you. In order to be able to do this, you will need to plan ahead to have your seal with you.

The cost for the booth rental will typically be two or three times the cost of similar space at a domestic show. Additionally, space in Latin America is measured in the metric system—typically multiple units of three meters by three meters. Your ten foot wide pop-up booth might be quite tight in a three meter wide space. It is also common to have several flood lights provided in your booth package that provide excellent lighting on your space.

If you purchase this type of exhibit space, your stand will not be bounded with pipes and curtains that are one meter high as is common in U.S. trade shows. The almost universal arrangement is a completely private space with two or three meter high walls and a full-height back that prohibits all access except from the front opening space. You will never know what is happening in your adjacent booths, and they will not know or see what you are doing. This is probably for security. Even so, never leave your booth unattended.

Exhibiting hours in Latin America will be very different from those at domestic shows. It is common to have trade shows open the exhibits for visitors at two or three in the afternoon and remain open until nine or ten p.m. Attendees and exhibitors at trade shows there are not nearly so focused on the theme of the show. Most product-based shows are very broad in their appeal. A telecommunications trade show will have exhibitors who launch rockets, sell radio transmitters, photocopiers, and computer hardware.

In most U.S. trade shows, companies are allowed to solicit only within their own booth space. This prohibition will probably not be enforced in Latin American countries. At most of the Latin American shows, a show attendee will be inundated with solicitations, product literature, and typical trade show promotional pieces in all the aisles as soon as one enters the exhibit areas.

After you have set up your exhibit, you might be expected to write out a detailed list of the items that will remain in your booth for the duration of the show. This would be signed by you, the exhibitor, as well as the security agent. He then places a security tape over your booth area. The theory is that he has an inventory on the items that are to remain in your booth, and then this will be checked as you tear down and leave the building, to make certain that no one takes any of your property during or after the show. I suspect that this encounter with security will be the last one that security will have with your specific booth. I recommend that you leave very few things of high value in the booth overnight, if they could be easily carted off. Take your portable computers with you each evening when you close down. Things seem to sprout legs when your booth is not being staffed.

There will probably be a bit more ceremony at the opening of the show than you would expect in the States. Local politicians as well as local business leaders are usually invited and presented. Their awesome prowess and herculean efforts described at these events might be somewhat inflated from reality. But, this ritual is still quite common. It is likely these people are important, but they also might be relevant to your expanding business. If you have the opportunity to meet any of them, always provide them with your business card.

You will make a good impression, should you have your display signs in Spanish (or Português if in Brazil). But, many educated professionals in Latin America are able to read English. Many people working in technology can read and understand English well, even if they do not speak it particularly well. Therefore, sales literature can be in English, but you will enhance your communication by having all your literature translated and printed in Spanish. Your company will be perceived as one who considers them important and values their culture. It was my practice to have business cards laid out and printed in Spanish. Another nice touch is to add QR (quick response) codes on the back of the card, that when scanned will take the inquirer directly to your website. Unless you clearly communicate to the contrary, they will probably infer that your products and customer support will also be in Spanish. If that is not the case, be certain to make that clear when you are talking with them and on your website.

By all means, have someone in your booth at all times who can speak the local language well on both on a conversational and technical level. Do not be surprised if visitors will want to try out their English with you. It might be perfect Queen's English, or it might be a bit rough to understand. Be welcoming. Remember, patience is a virtue.

Have more business cards that you can imagine to distribute freely. They are cheap advertising. Oftentimes, the person standing in your booth might not be the decision-maker. The boss might have sent some of his staff on a mission to find out information on his behalf. For many years, I have posed this question to booth visitors, "Who along with you will make a the final decision about a purchase?" The body language of those visiting your booth will answer that question, if the boss is with them. If the decision-maker is someone else, give your visitor a couple of extra business cards and ask him to pass them along to the boss. You might write a personal note to the boss on the back of the card. Ask for the boss's name and contact information. You will want to follow-up with an email to him as well as everyone who visits you in your booth.

In the States, most attendees at trade shows tend to walk down the aisle and look at your booth out of the corner of their eyes bashfully and not wanting to be approached directly. They tend to create distance between you and them by remaining in the aisle. If you are talking with another staff person in your booth, they might well pass by your booth and not enter. In Latin America, the body language is totally different. Show visitors typically stop in the aisle and read aloud every word on your display. They often enter your booth area and examine each item on display. If you are talking with another perspective customer, they will usually wait patiently for you to finish your conversation, perhaps even listening to what you are describing. Recall what I wrote earlier about the physical proximity of Latinos when they are talking to you in person. If they have an interest in your products, they will ask you many questions.

If they are not working in your professional field, they might ask you a question or two about exactly what you do, to confirm that your products are not of interest to them. They will then thank you kindly for the opportunity to see your booth and then move on. Out of courtesy, they might ask for a business card to pass on to some colleague they know. You will always want to hand them two or three cards. There are always qualified buyers of your products and services who will not be at the show. These good people might be a possible source of referral to a friend.

The exhibitors' booths furnishings in Latin American shows will frequently be just like they are at trade shows in the United States. Often, exhibitors install large screen televisions, spouting off information in English. Latin American exhibitors sometimes construct elaborate single-use show booths. They may be incredibly more labor intensive than you would ever see at home. They sometimes construct multilevel floors or even complete multiple room booths with open walls to show off the products. Incredible, complex geometric designs of tubing, glass, and even large items not particularly related to the products, such as aquariums, park benches with cobble stone walkways, and flower gardens may be included. Many exhibitors staff their booths with beautiful models and provide every interested man with a souvenir photograph taken with these women.

One thing was a great surprise to me. I knew that my small American company would spend ten to twenty thousand dollars to travel to and exhibit in a particular Latin American trade show. I did not expect to find that some countries, particularly from Asia, charter a large airliner and provide round-trip transportation, shipping and government paid booth space to exhibitors from their country. Their view is that this is an economic stimulus toward the exportation of their goods. I have never expected or received any of this type of assistance from the United States government.

I commend to you a book I have written, *Secrets for a Successful Small Business: What the University Will Not Teach You*. This helpful book goes into much detail about trade show exhibition as well as many issues confronting the small business owner. Many of the details presented there would apply to Latin America as much as they do in the United States.

ExpoComm in Caracas, Venezuela

I exhibited at a large trade show in Venezuela several times. On one of my trips there, I arrived at the exhibit area of the *Poliedro de Caracas* to set up at what was probably the country's largest telecommunications and information trade show. I arrived early in the afternoon so that I could install our portable trade show booth and quickly return to my hotel to do some planning for follow-up after the show. I was pleased that my badge was properly prepared in advance and ready for pickup. When I entered the large sports complex, I noticed that it had been converted into an excellent venue for a large trade show attendance. I was especially pleased to feel both the reduction of temperature and humidity due to the surprising fact that they were running the air conditioning for setup. This would be the exception to the norm in the States except at Las Vegas.

As my colleague and I entered the building with our cases of equipment, the security guard told us that the elevators were not working and that we would have to carry our crates up several flights of stairs. We climbed a vertical rise of approximately forty feet with everything. We then began to look for that special booth space for which I had paid a handsome fee to exhibit for the four days. All the booths had numbers clearly marked with the company name in clear black letters over the entrance of the booth. All were marked except ours. There was a small sheet of notebook paper taped to the back of the stand that identified our particular space. This would be covered up when we install our booth furnishings, which has a large sign with our company name. As I looked around, it became obvious that the booth spaces were not necessarily ordered consecutively with the assigned booth numbers. The numbers seemed to increase as you went one direction and generally decreased when going the other, but not necessarily. For that reason, I decided to ask that they install the nameplate that we had ordered for the show, to make our booth appearance consistent with the others at the show.

I located the exhibitors desk and asked for the floor manager. She was not around. The gringo show manager came by shortly to see if everything was all right. I told him of the concern. He said they remembered our large sign from the previous year, and they did not want to cover any of it up. Therefore, they did not install the sign. He said that it was made, available, and could be installed if we wished. I told him to proceed with the installation.

Several hours later, I saw the floor manager, and she began looking for the sign. She found it across the aisle from us, between two other booths. I was happy to see that it contained both our company name, properly spelled, and our correct booth number. She said that she would have a worker install it immediately. Since we had completed our installation, we decided to head back to the hotel, being assured that all would be ready for the start of the show at two p.m. the next afternoon.

In an abundance of caution, the next day we arrived at the hall about an hour before the scheduled opening for the show, because exhibit hours are a little more flexible in Latin America than in the states. We thought that attendees might be admitted early. We were correct. When we arrived, many people were roaming the exhibit areas. Our sign had not been installed. I notified the floor manager again that we still wanted the sign.

Later that afternoon, one of the show managers checked in with me. Without a spoken word, I simply pointed up to the location where the sign was to have been installed. He uttered something under his breath and then told me that he was promised that it would be up by that morning. The entire first day of exhibiting passed without our sign. We went through the identical litany the next morning when the sign was not yet installed. Finally, a gentleman showed up with some metal framework that he wanted to use to mount the sign. Since it was much wider than our booth space, he had to return to his maintenance area to locate a mounting that was only three meters wide to cover the front of our booth. By midway through the show, we assisted the laborer to install the sign that had been staring at us from across the aisle two and one half days. I learned that in Spanish, the word *inmediatamente* (immediately) does not imply the urgency or speed of action that you would expect in the States. Its connotation is similar to the word soon.

If I had not been persistent, it would have never been installed. Everyone had the greatest intentions to solve our problem, agreed to do it, even on a specified time table. Each person with whom we dealt was friendly and courteous. It just did not get done until we kept surfacing the issue again and again. Assertiveness is sometimes needed, but patience is a virtue. Plan ahead.

Despite these delays, the show was a great success for my company. We met a number of our customers that we had previously known only through phone calls and emails. We also reached a number of new prospective customers with whom we would follow-up in the near future.

Part 5
Relationships are Paramount

Strong Values within the Latino Culture

There are a number of strong values that are widespread in the Latin American culture. Some of these values will be in contrast to what is the common practice in the United States. While broad generalizations do not apply to all individuals, they are important to grasp and embrace if you wish to cross the culture gap into the Latin culture. I will discuss four specific areas here.

Family—Decisions are often made out of a sense of consensus. Big decisions are not generally made by individuals without consulting the family. Family does not mean only the nuclear family, but one's extended family including kids, parents, and grandparents and even close friends who might not be blood related. Ongoing emotional and financial support for all those in the family is important and will be a factor in any major decisions that are made. In America we highly value independence in thinking, finances, and in behavior. Latinos are much more interdependent in their families and decision-making. If you are tempted to see this as co-dependence, you would be mistaken. There is a strong desire to see that each person is recognized and valued in the decision-making on big issues. Being personally connected to one's family is a foundational value within the Latino culture.

Hierarchy and Formality—Each person is expected to defer to those who are in authority because of age, gender, title, and economic status. Professional titles are important and widely used when talking to others. In conversations, professional titles often take precedent over family titles. For example, a wife might say, "The doctor or the professor..." rather than "My husband..." Deference is quite common with many people. Decision-making will take into significant account the preferences by those who are in authority. This will include the parents and grandparents. At work, it would always include one's immediate supervisor and long-standing company policies. Confrontation of one's superiors is virtually unheard of.

Relationships—When you encounter someone, asking about the health and happiness of one's family is often the first topic of conversation, even at a business meeting. Be prepared to share this information about yourself and your family. Have your family photographs in your wallet to share when the need arises. Inquire about their family as well. This interaction is important.

Schedules and important tasks to complete are less important than being polite and courteous. Latinos want you to be happy, and they strive to provide an atmosphere where happiness is the norm. Being in a hurry, detached, and impersonal treatment is considered rude. When someone wants to be excused, they might use the expression, *"Con su permiso."* Literally translated it would mean "with your permission." It is not really asking anyone's permission. But the phrase is simply acknowledging that you are present and that you are recognized by them.

Insisting that one is right or blaming others is not considered being polite. Clutching or monitoring your cell phone during an in-person conversation will imply you to be rude and send the message that your conversation with that person is not important. Being business-like does not mean to be particularly efficient or impersonal. It means to be attentive and respectful.

Accept what is—Take each day as it comes. Time is flexible, so punctuality and deadlines give way to living fully in the present moment. Learn to value the experience of living in the present moment. Order and fixed procedures are not critical agendas. Be engaged in the conversation with the persons you are with, not all the other persons you need to address. A saying that is all too true is, "Most people listen to someone in order to respond. It is much better to listen to understand what they are saying." I believe this is true with many Americans, but listening in order to respond rather than learning is a part of our downgrading of our relationships. Be a great listener. We all desire to be known, even if others do not agree with us. Patience is a virtue.

Expanding Your Friendships

A great deal of this book will help you understand and enter into the Latino world as you travel out of the your country. This section, however, will challenge you to build relationships with Latinos you can meet and get to know at home. Much of what I have presented elsewhere in this book will also apply to our newly developed friendships with Latinos here. None of us want to be treated as invisible when others encounter us. We want to be recognized, respected, and welcomed and be given the safe space to be ourselves. I encourage you to make a point to treat all people this way. These values form much of the bedrock of all healthy relationships. Racial arrogance can be so subtle—even falsely justified, when we focus on ourselves and our preferences at the expense of others. Hopefully, we are all people in progress—progressing to build communities that listen to one another more than ones who are talking about or to the sojourners that we have in our midst.

Having a good friend is a great thing. Sometimes our friendships occur naturally with little effort on our part. More commonly, the building of a great friendship can be work over a long time. Many of us are most comfortable being with people who look, act, think, and feel just like we do. We like to stay well within our comfort zone. When we commit to meet, know, and welcome into our lives someone who is different from us, we take a big step forward in growing up in our personal relationships. Building and crossing a cultural bridge to enlarge our circle of friendships will generally happen only as we take initiative to do so. I hope that you will build such a bridge.

The Bible guides us in how to treat people in our midst. The Old Testament prophet Zechariah delivered this message from the Lord: "This is what the Lord of Heaven's Armies says: Judge fairly, and show mercy and kindness to one another. Do not oppress widows, orphans, foreigners, and the poor. And do not scheme against each other" (Zech 7:9-10 NLT). Selective oppression (think rejection) is not to be the practice of God-fearers. This was God's message to ancient Israel: "O people, the Lord has told you what is good, and this is what he requires of you: to do what is right, to love mercy, and to walk humbly with your God" (Micah 6:8). The writer of the book of Proverbs brings us this exhortation, "Do not withhold good from those who deserve it when it's in your power to help them. If you can help your neighbor now, don't say 'Come back tomorrow, and then I'll help you'" (Proverbs 3:27-28). The author of the Gospel of Luke similarly writes, "Do to others as you would like them to do to you" (Luke 6:31). While these writings span many hundreds of years and were written several thousand years ago, the values they espouse are still wisdom for how we should treat one another today. We are asked to be kind, merciful, fair-minded, and helpful to others that we might not know well and whose life-experience is quite different from our own.

Sometimes Anglos may feel tempted to treat Latinos as visitors and "reach out" to them or try to help them and love them as neighbors. But without realizing it, even in well-intentioned situations many times the majority culture expect to set the tone on their own terms for how the outreach "to minorities" should be conducted. If, on the other hand, you take the initiative to engage in an established Latino community, they can welcome visitors on their own terms. Hispanic churches and countless Latino civic, educational, and cultural organizations present an endless opportunity to do this. A reciprocity in trust and learning can develop out of these genuine relationships.

They can learn to trust you as an individual and hopefully in time invite you to get to know their extended family.

Even if your Spanish language skills are limited, learn to correctly pronounce their name in Spanish—both their first and last names. Speak intelligently about their country of origin. Bear in mind that many of these people are already Americans, so do not treat them as a visitor to our country. Many Latinos you encounter here are citizens and possibly are a second or third generation Americans, who have chosen to continue to frame their lives out of the traditions of their families and have not embraced all the so called "American lifestyle." Understand that their American heritage might be quite different from one's own American heritage which stems from western European heritage.

Value their culture and respect their traditions. Approach Latinos with the same respect that you desire having come from your own cultural background. By being friends with people who are different from who we are, we are setting ourselves up for not only further understanding about culture and language, but also for a gradual healing of the barriers of brokenness that divide many of us as humans.

I would also suggest two additional books written by me that will apply well in our friendships with Latinos, although the ideas put forth are not specific only to Latino friends. *Great Connections: Loving with Limits* discusses the importance of establishing and respecting healthy boundaries in order to have a great relational connection with others. *Forgiveness: Unleashing a Transformational Process* presents the idea that strong reconciled friendships must be preceded by forgiveness and the absence of retaliation toward those who have hurt us or who are simply different from us. In many ways, healthy friendships with everyone will have a lot of common values put forth in these two books.

Part 6
Commencement Exercises

Graduation

Bridging the culture gap between the American and Latin America is not an event, but rather an ongoing process. As you make the investment of time and money to learn, travel, experiment, and welcome new friends into your life, I suggest that you organize your learning, contacts, and vocabulary into meaningful resources. Record your thoughts, questions, and experiences in some sort of journal for future review and reference. You should probably do this daily if you are out of the country. After returning to your routine at home, you will have many conflicting demands on your time. Unless you are superhuman, sometimes urgent demands can take precedence over the highest long-term priority items. Learning from and appreciating a different culture is a life-long and valuable investment.

When traveling internationally–especially for business, it is common to go to the capital city, stay in American hotels, enjoy the hotel Wi-Fi, receive pay-per-view movies and American news networks, and sometimes even our major domestic entertainment television networks at the push of a button on the remote control. We enjoy a hot shower and eat in one of the hotel's fine restaurants. We exit this normal environment only for our business meetings, show participation, and then finally fly back to our homes and resume life just as before we left.

I invite you to upgrade your experience beyond this myopic living. Do some research on the country's history and government before you leave home. On each visit to Latin

America, decide to experience several events there that you could not experience at home. When you arrive, talk with the local residents. Ride their subways. Go see some of their museums and parks. Shop in a few retail stores. Visit their ancient ruins. Plan an extra day or two to do some of these things you could only do there. Discover again that American history is not the same as United States history.

It is gratifying to know that a *Bolívar* (currency in Venezuela) carries a historical reference to Simón Bolívar—the liberator who was born in Caracas but influenced what is now Colombia and Panama. Discover the secret place where a statue to Lázaro Cárdenas, an early president of Mexico is located in Caracas. Know that Lázaro Cárdenas is also a city near the Pacific in the state of Michoacán in Mexico. The man for whom the city was named was the President of Mexico and a great benefactor to Venezuela.

Learn that the two main telecommunication satellites orbiting the Earth replaced a few years ago were Morelos One and Two. They were specifically named after Morelos, a former president of Mexico. Learn that the Hotel Soledad in Morelia, Mexico, around the corner from the cathedral, has no one on staff who can speak English. Learn that the hotel installs a thirty-foot high crystal chandelier over the atrium fountain during the Christmas season, and that the building was constructed in 1735 to be a monastery. Know what it is like to sing in Spanish with a thousand other worshipers at an 8 p.m. Sunday mass in a cathedral whose construction began one hundred years before the United States was a nation. Discover *medallones con limón* (beef medallions with lime) at Harry's Bar in Mexico City. Learn that while all three countries speak Spanish, Mexico has *albercas* while Venezuela has *piscinas*; Argentina has *piletas*. We call them all swimming pools.

Learn that Mexico City has a population greater than New York City or Los Angeles. The metropolitan area around Mexico City is approximately twenty-one million people. The *Templo Mayor* was built in the 14th century in honor of the Aztec god of war and god of water. Immediately adjacent is the Roman Catholic Cathedral constructed over three centuries (1573-1813). Both are important places to see in person. They are located on the *Zócolo,* the very large square or plaza in Mexico City, where the centers of government for both the city and the nation are located. The mammoth mosaic murals on the outside walls of the central library at the National Autonomous University of Mexico are an architectural treasure and simply breathtaking. They depict the vast history of their country.

Learn that you can seldom be served *"té helado"* except in American restaurants. *"Té helado"* is unknown in parts of South America, even where *"te frío"* (iced tea) is widely served. Also expect to be served only about eight ounces in your glass and that you might be charged again and again for each refill. *Té negro* (black tea) to one country is *té caliente* (hot tea) in another.

Learn where you can see and pet the donkey that drinks thirty bottles of beer and pop daily right from the bottle. Also learn how the Aztecs used the maguey plant to make an alcoholic drink called pulque, writing parchment, soap, a needle and thread, and fabric. Taste, see, and feel all of this without paying a gate admission fee at the base of the two-thousand year old Great Pyramids of the Sun and Moon just forty kilometers northeast of Mexico City. When you climb the steps to the tops of these two structures, you will wonder how they were constructed without the help of modern construction equipment. The steps you climb are uneven and not at all compliant with OSHA (Occupational Safety and Health

Administration) standards that are required in the United States, but they have served well for thousands of years.

If you want to practice your Spanish you should go to Cozumel rather than Cancun. While you are on the island enjoy some authentic key lime pie after a hard day of diving in the incredible reefs where two-hundred feet visibility is typical. The place to stay in Cozumel is the Playa Azul, a small Mexican-owned hotel, with an amazing beach and attentive and personable staff. By all means, be certain you are in Cozumel on a Sunday night. They always have a fantastic party on the plaza downtown. There are live bands, dancing, lots of people, and local artists who have their unique works for sale.

If you enjoy music, purchase compact disks of *"música nacional"* wherever you go. You will have recordings of mariachi bands, symphonic works, and culturally based music and artists which will truly make your collection unique.

Depending upon how you ask a question, learn that a "yes" given in response to a simple "yes or no question" usually means, "I agree with your question or frustrations"—not necessarily a confirmation on which corner the Banamex office is located. That market that is "just across from the big fountain outside the metro station" can easily be two or three blocks away from the station when you come up from the metro. Learn to check with two, three or four people when making a decision about the directions to a specific location. Many people tend to tell you what they think you want to hear. This is especially true when trying to find a particular location in a city while on foot.

I now feel quite at home in some of these wonderful places. After traveling throughout Latin America for many years, I have developed several close friendships with people who live there. We phone, text, and email each other as if we lived in the same town. It is as if the distance between us has been erased.

Embracing a culture that is different from our own is an ongoing effort, but one with great personal satisfaction and fulfillment.

Accept the wisdom that whether you are abroad or building a relationship with a Latino friend who lives here in the States, that it is always our responsibility to take the initiative to enter into and value their world. Away, we are the guest, and at home we are the gracious host striving to be welcoming. When we show appreciation of who someone is, we are building a foundation of long-term trust and personal confidence that can draw our friendships much closer. When someone is valued, they will often extend a high value back to those people who have treated them well.

As you learn to live better in the present moment, you will have fewer and fewer criticisms of those practices that are different from yours. There are two important golden threads that are woven through every chapter of this book. Live out of them as you travel and also at home. Always remember that patience is a virtue, and always plan ahead. As you move toward enjoying more of the Latin American culture, I trust that you will find it as rewarding as I have. I close with the words of a popular Spanish phrase spoken as good friends travel apart, *"Vaya con Dios, mi amigo."*

Suggested Resources

Ellis, Larry D. *Great Connections: Loving with Limits*. Denver, Colorado: Adoration Publishing Company, 2018.

____. *Forgiveness:Unleashing a Transformational Process*. Denver, Colorado: Adoration Publishing Company, 2010.

____. *Secrets For a Successful Small Business*. Denver, Colorado: Adoration Publishing Company, 2011.

Keenan, Joseph J. *Breaking Out of Beginner's Spanish*. Austin, Texas: University of Texas Press, 1994.

Pierson, Raymond H. *Guide to Spanish Idioms*. New York: McGraw-Hill Education, 1985.

Spanish for Dummies. Hoboken, New Jersey: John Wiley & Sons, Inc., 2012, (laminated pages).